The Ultra Guitar Songbook

ISBN-13: 978-1-4234-2770-4
ISBN-10: 1-4234-2770-X

7777 W. BLUEMOUND RD. P.O. BOX 13819 MILWAUKEE, WI 53213

Visit Hal Leonard Online at
www.halleonard.com

The Ultra Guitar Songbook

Bad Moon Rising

Words and Music by John Fogerty

Gtrs. 1, 4 & 5: Tune down 1 step:
(low to high) D-G-C-F-A-D

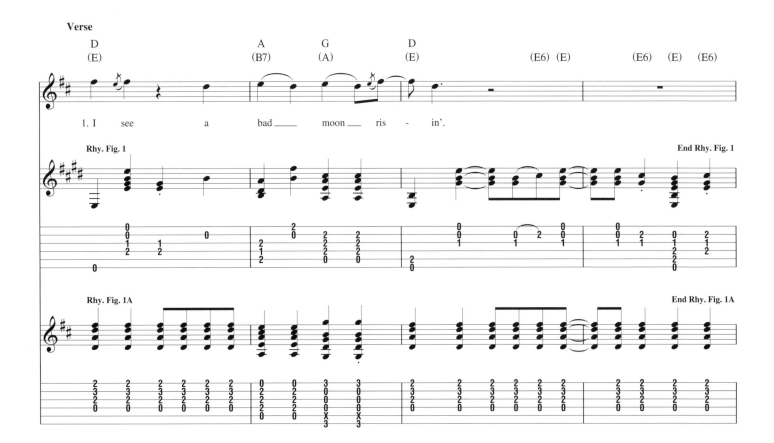

*Symbols in parentheses represent chord names respective to detuned guitars.
Symbols above reflect actual sounding chords.

Gtr. 1: w/ Rhy. Fig. 1 (3 times)
Gtrs. 2 & 3: w/ Rhy. Fig. 1A (3 times)

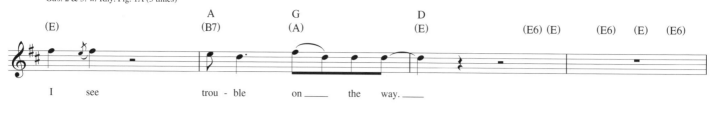

I see trou - ble on ____ the way. ____

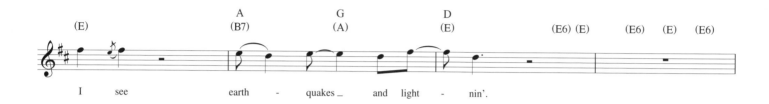

I see earth - quakes ___ and light - nin'.

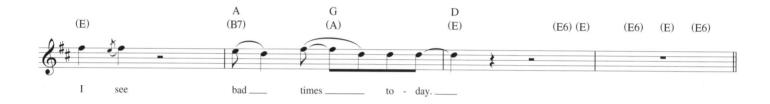

I see bad ___ times _____ to - day. ____

Chorus

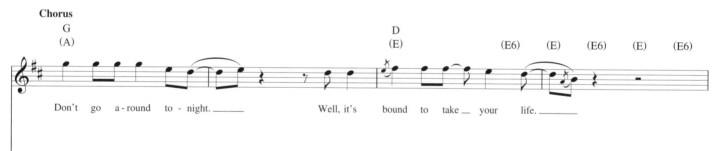

Don't go a - round to - night. _____ Well, it's bound to take ___ your life. _____

Gtr. 1   **Rhy. Fig. 2**

Gtrs. 2 & 3   **Rhy. Fig. 2A**

Gtr. 1: w/ Rhy. Fig. 2
Gtrs. 2 & 3: w/ Rhy. Fig. 2A
Gtr. 4 tacet

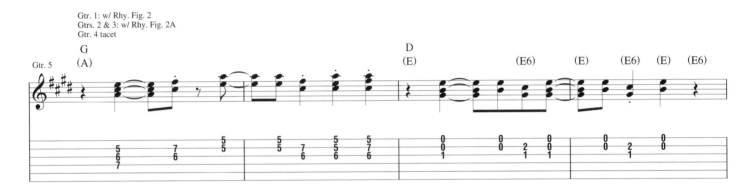

Verse

Gtr. 1: w/ Rhy. Fig. 1 (4 times)
Gtrs. 2 & 3: w/ Rhy. Fig. 1A (4 times)
Gtr. 5 tacet

3. Hope you got your things to - geth - er.

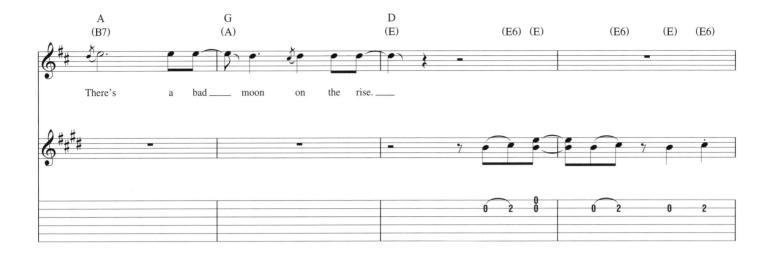

There's a bad ___ moon on the rise. ___

Don't come a-round to-night. ___ Well, it's bound to take ___ your life. ___

There's a bad ___ moon on the rise. ___

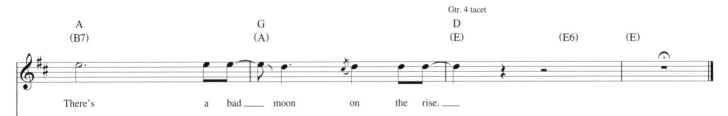

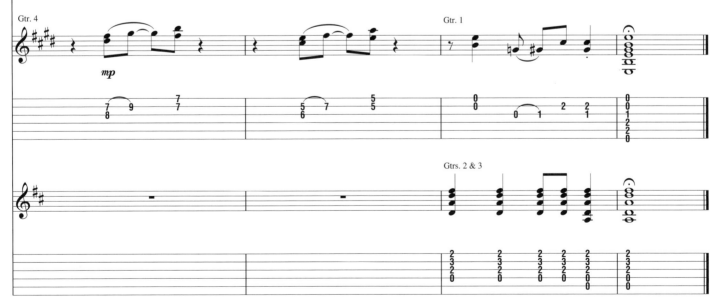

Creep

**Words and Music by Albert Hammond, Mike Hazlewood, Thomas Yorke,
Richard Greenwood, Philip Selway, Colin Greenwood and Edward O'Brian**

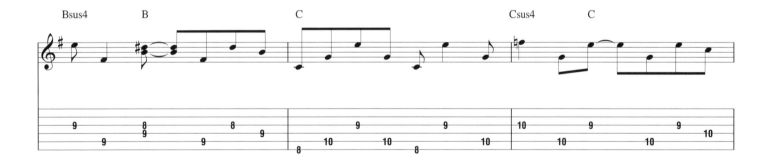

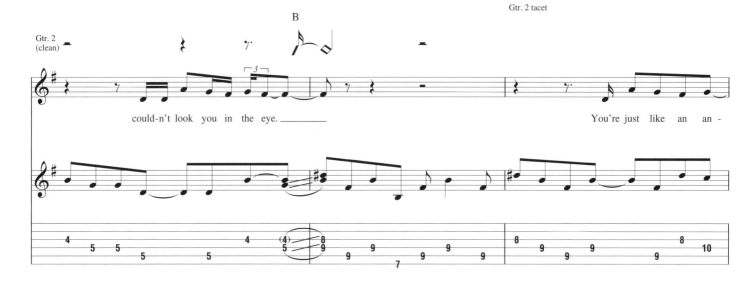

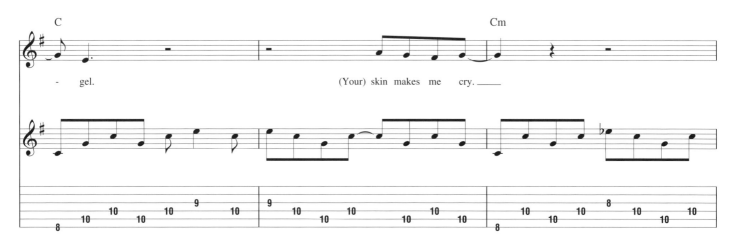

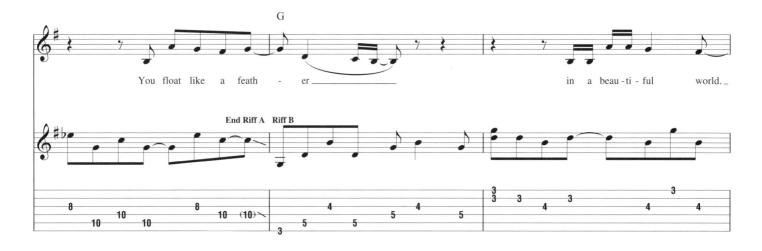

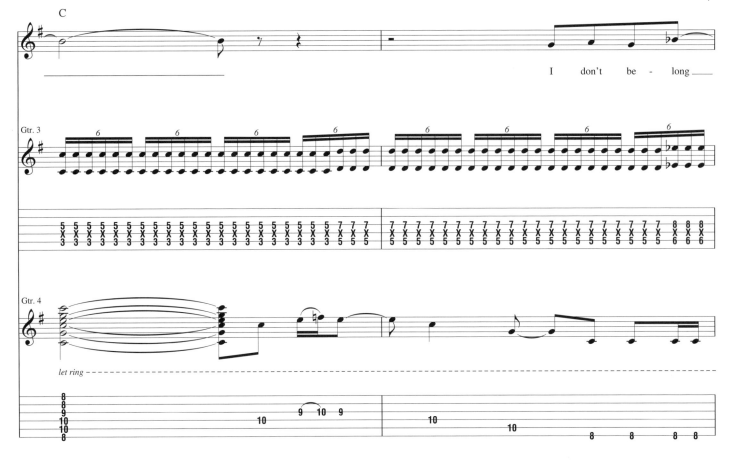

I don't be - long ____

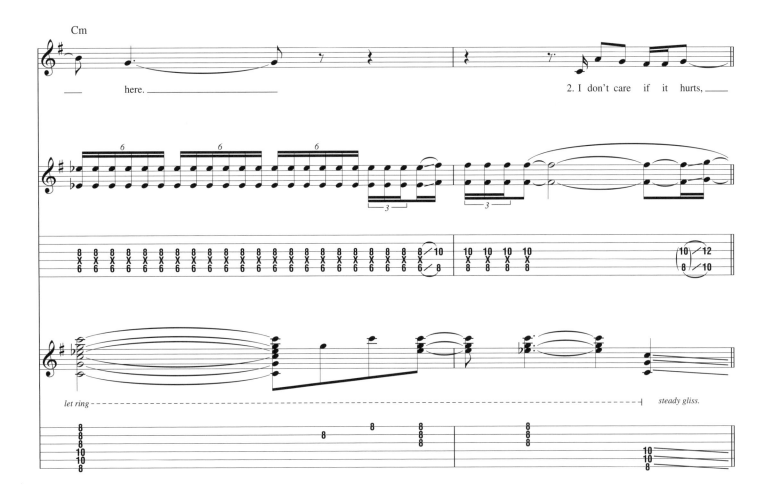

____ here. ____

2. I don't care if it hurts, ____

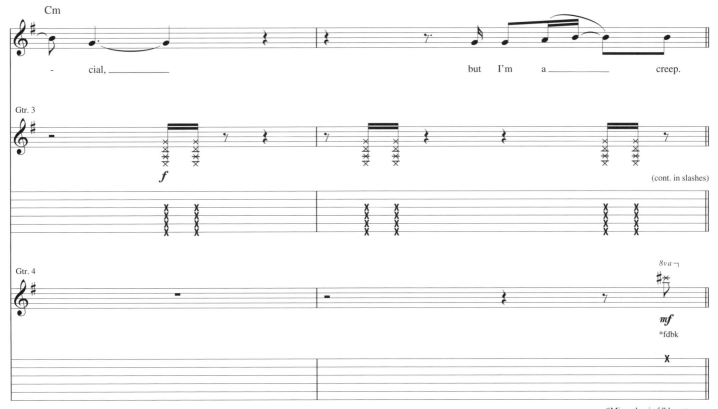

*Microphonic fdbk, not
caused by string vibration.

 Coda

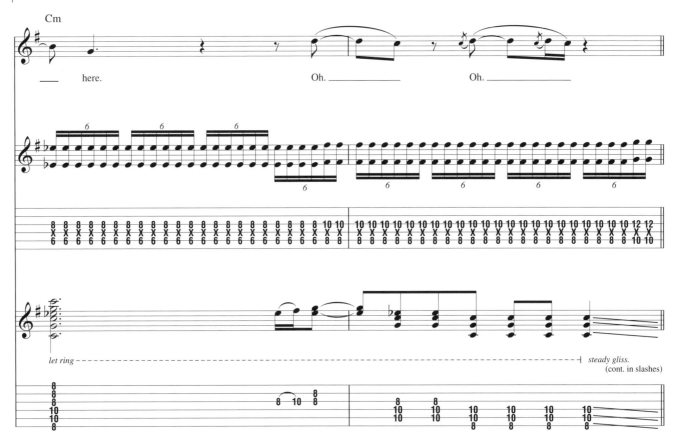

Bridge

G

Rhy. Fig. 1

Gtr. 4

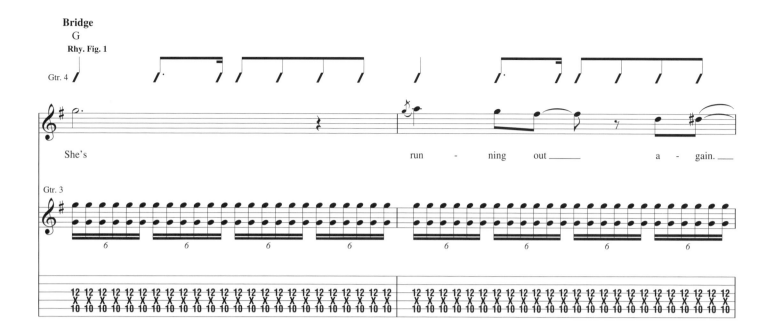

She's run - ning out ____ a - gain. ____

Gtr. 3

B^{type2}

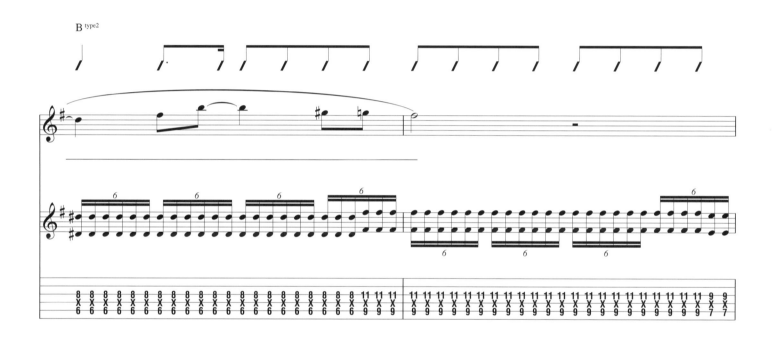

C

End Rhy. Fig. 1

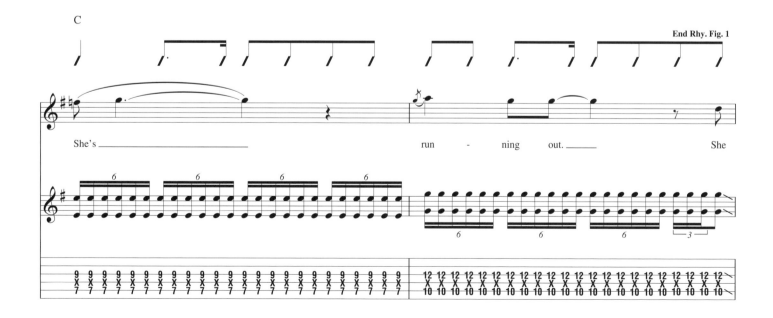

She's _____ run - ning out. ____ She

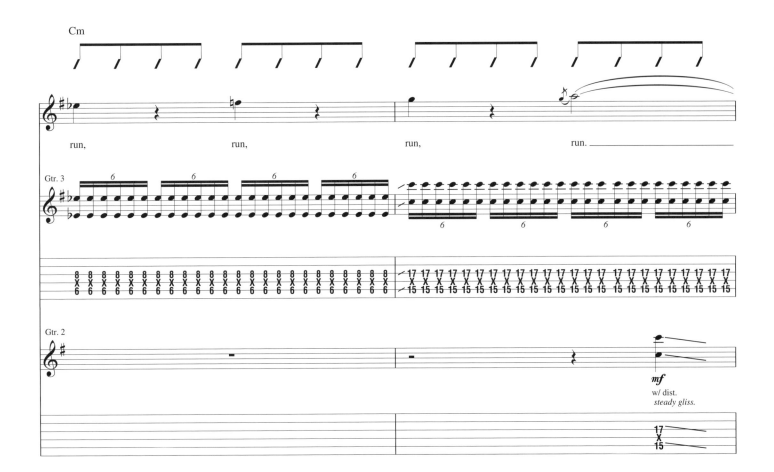

run,   run,   run,   run. _____

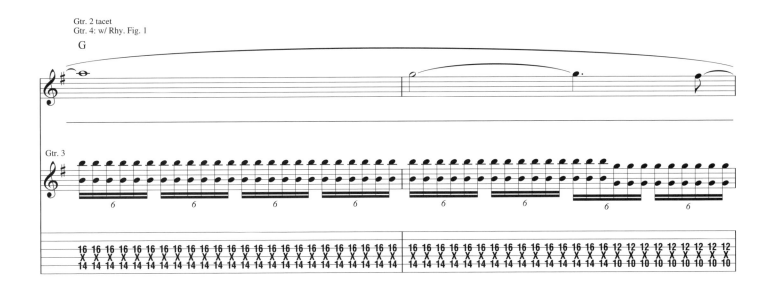

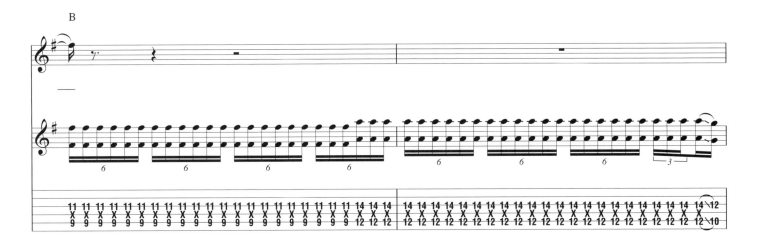

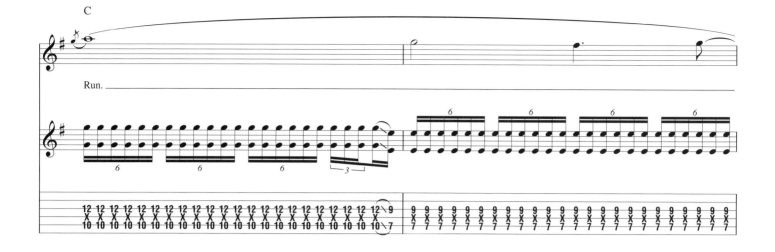

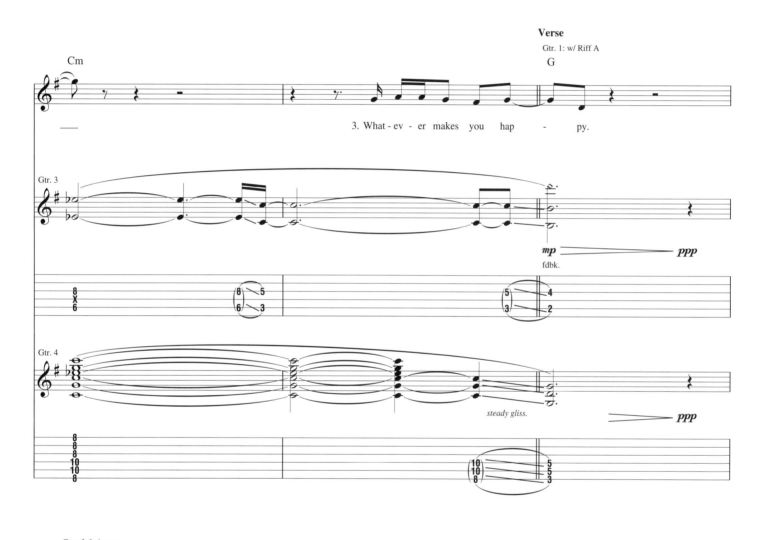

Verse

Gtr. 1: w/ Riff A

3. What-ev-er makes you hap - py.

What-ev-er you want. ___ You're so fuck-ing spe -

- cial.   I wish I was spe - cial,

Outro-Chorus

Gtr. 1: w/ Riff B (1st 6 meas.)

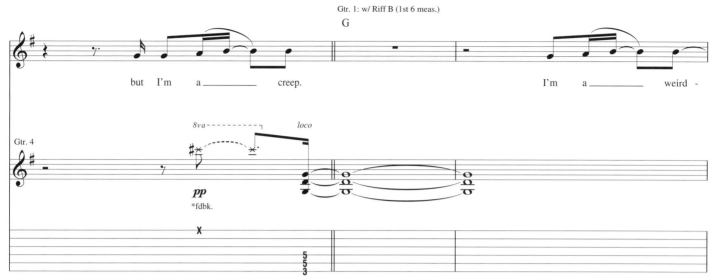

but I'm a _____ creep. I'm a _____ weird-

*Microphonic fdbk., not caused by string vibration.

-o. _____ What the hell am I do - ing here? ___

I don't be - long ___ here. I don't be - long ___ here.

Dani California

Words and Music by Anthony Kiedis, Flea, John Frusciante and Chad Smith

*Two gtrs. arr. for one.
**Chord symbols reflect overall harmony.

***Gtr. 2 (clean), *mf.* Composite arrangement

G   Dm   Am

What in the world does your com-pa-ny take ___ me for?

Verse

*Gtr. 1: w/ Rhy. Fig. 1 (2 times)   Gtr. 2 tacet

Am   G   Dm   Am

2. Black ban-dan-na, sweet ___ Lou-i-si-an-a, rob-bin' on a bank ___ in the state of In-di-an-a.

*Modular filter off

G   Dm   Am

She's a run-ner, reb-el, and a stun-ner, on her mer-ry way, ___ say-in', "Ba-by, what-cha gon-na?"

G   Dm   Am   G

Look-ing down the bar-rel of a hot met-al for-ty-five. Just an-oth-er way to sur-vive. ___

Riff A   **End Riff A**

**Gtrs. 1 & 2

w/ modular filter

**Composite arrangement

Verse

Gtr. 1: w/ Rhy. Fig. 1 (2 times)

Am   G   Dm   Am

4. Push the fad - er, gift - ed an - i - ma - tor one ___ for the now ___ and e - lev - en for the lat - er.

Gtr. 2

Gtr. 4
divisi
phase shifter off

G   Dm   Am

Nev - er made it up ___ to Min - ne - so - ta, North Da - ko - ta man ___ was a gun - nin' for the quo - ta.

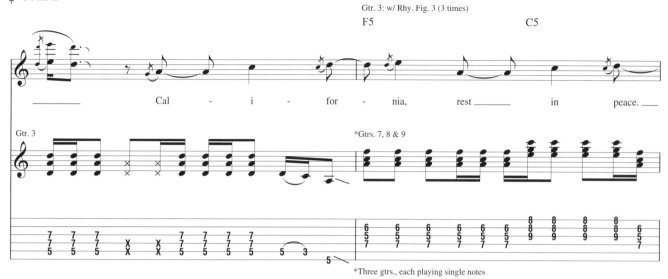

Coda 2

Gtr. 3: w/ Rhy. Fig. 3 (3 times)

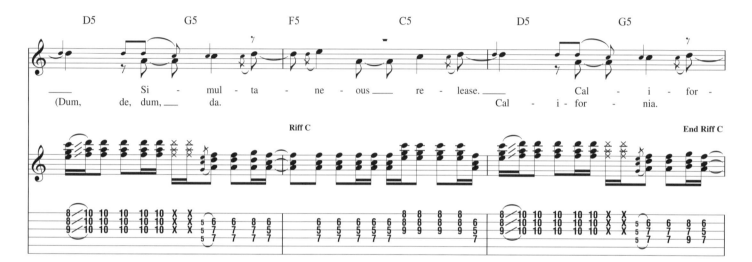

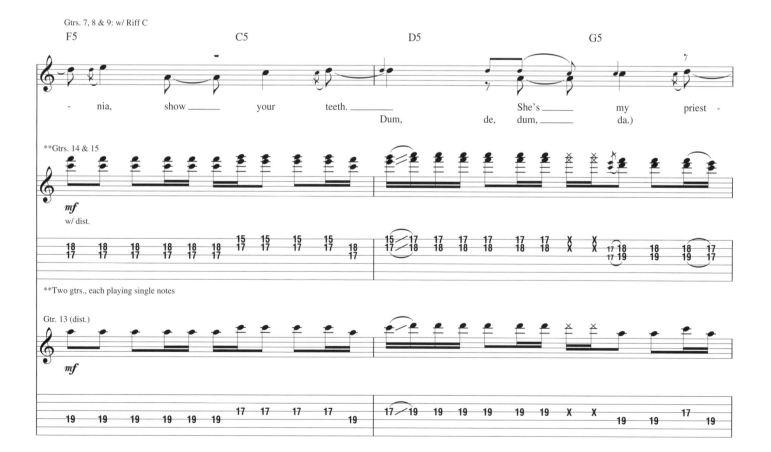

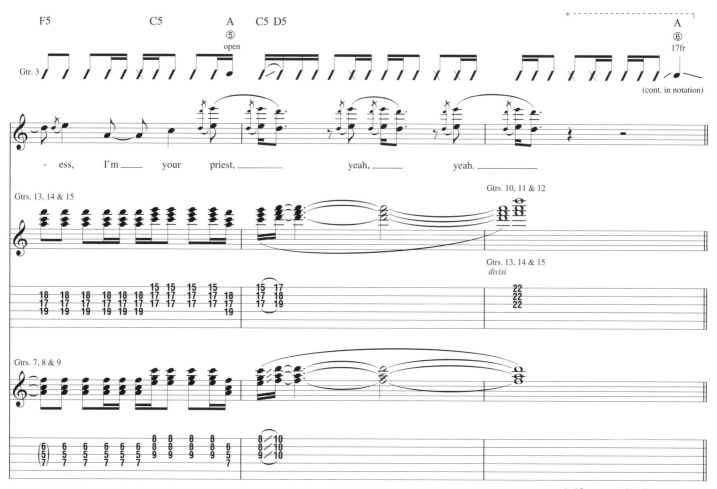

-ess, I'm _____ your priest, _____ yeah, _____ yeah. _____

*w/ flanger on entire mix

Outro-Guitar Solo

Gtrs. 7 - 15 tacet

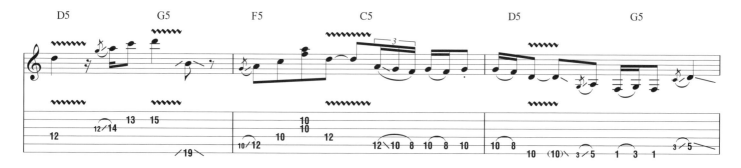

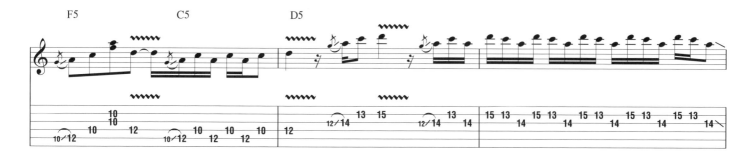

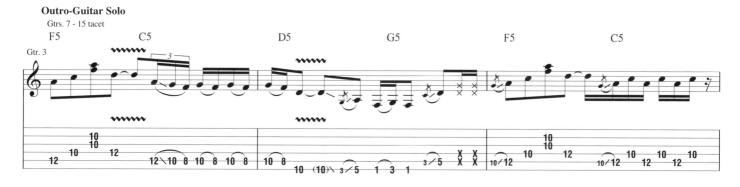

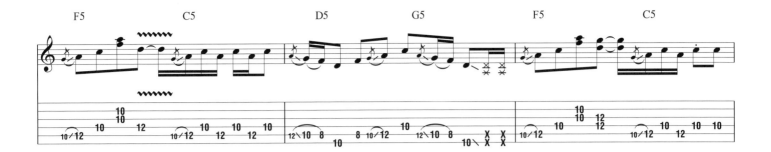

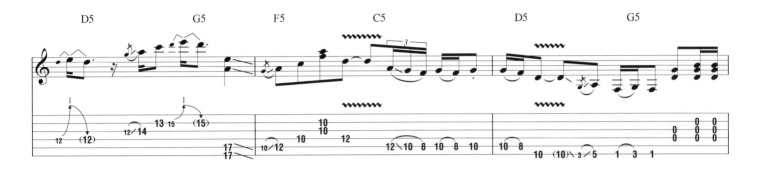

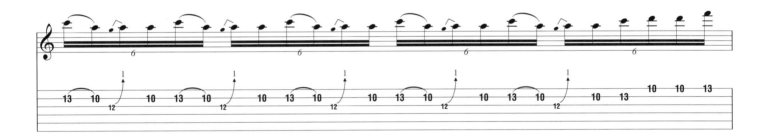

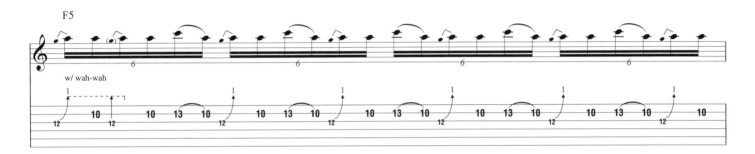

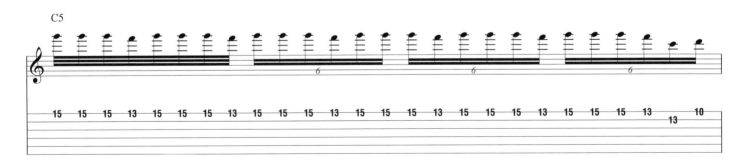

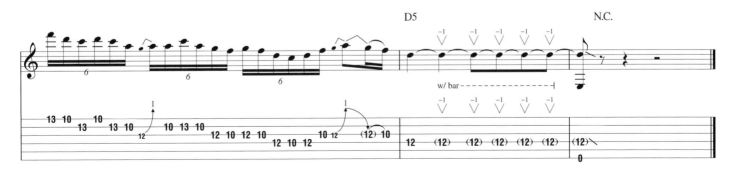

Hollywood Nights

Words and Music by Bob Seger

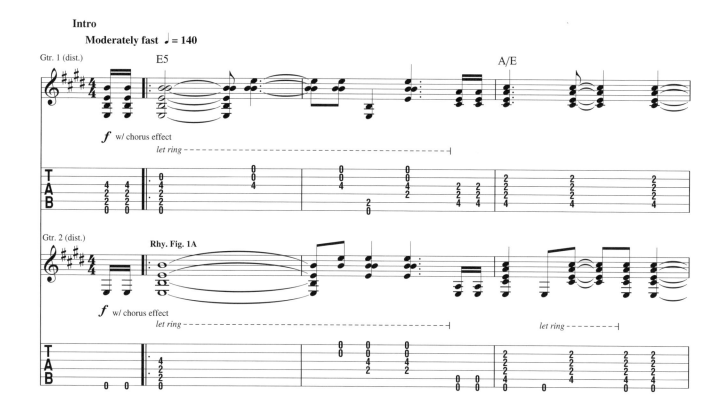

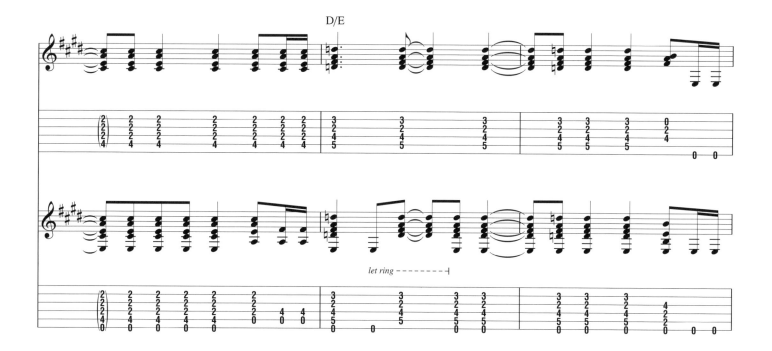

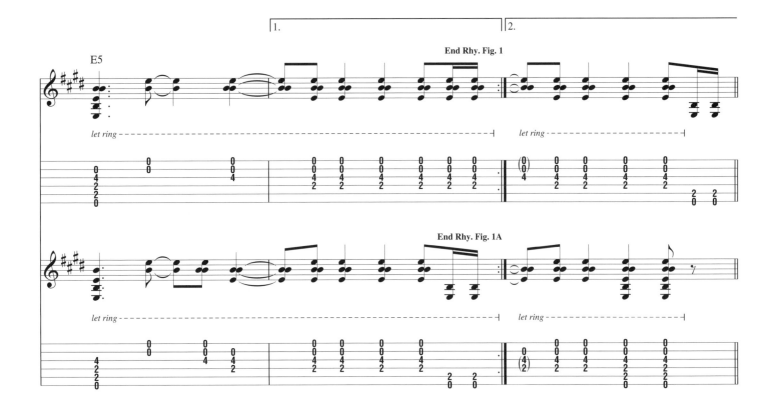

1. She stood there bright as the sun on that Cal - i - for - nia coast.
3. He'd head - ed west 'cause he felt that a change would do ___ him good.

He was a Mid - west - ern boy on his
See some old friends; good for the

own.
soul.

End Rhy. Fig. 2

End Rhy. Fig. 2A

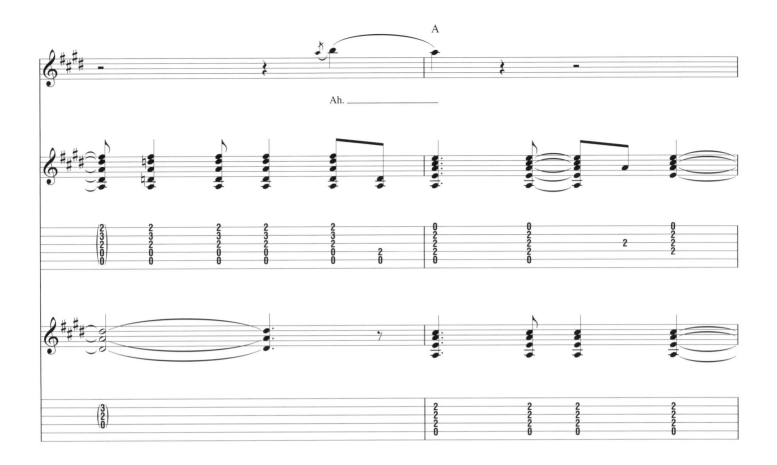

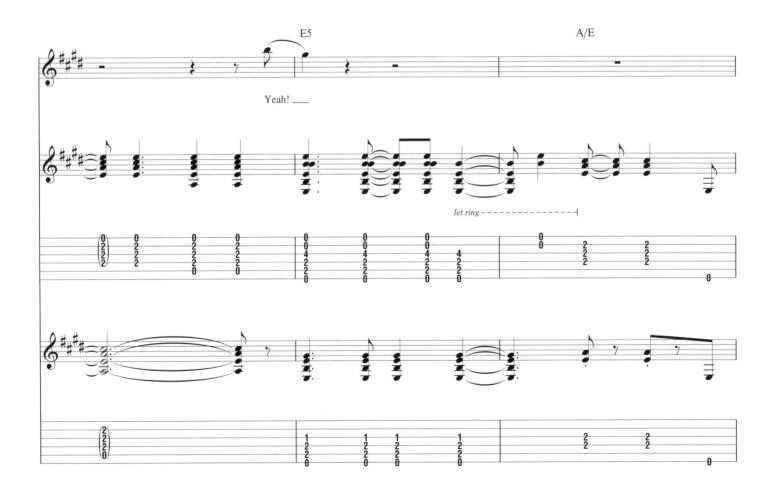

E5

Ow.

let ring

P.M.

let ring

slight P.M.

D.S. al Coda

Mm. ___

P.M.

slight P.M.

Hot for Teacher

Words and Music by David Lee Roth, Edward Van Halen and Alex Van Halen

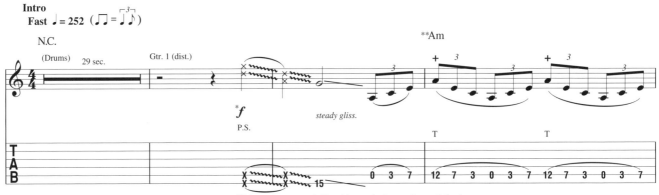

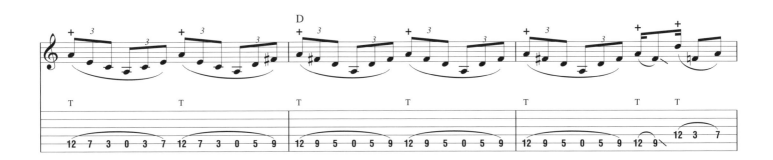

*Pickup selector set to bridge pickup, w/ vol. control set to full vol.

**Chord symbols reflect implied harmony.

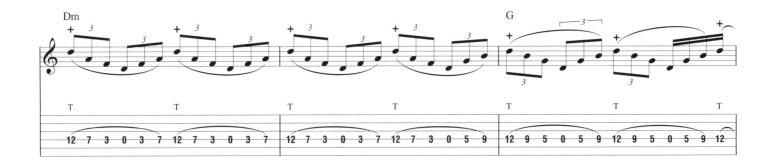

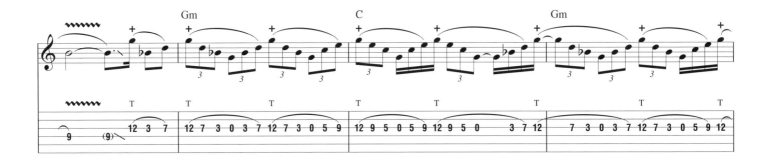

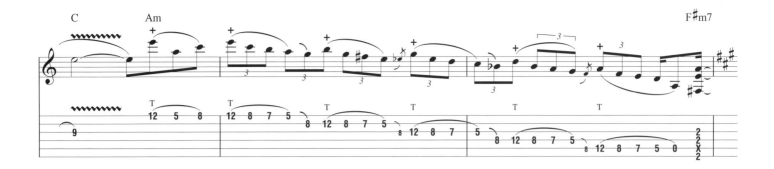

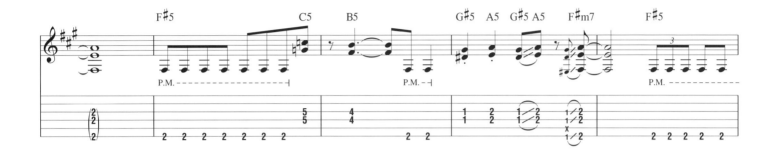

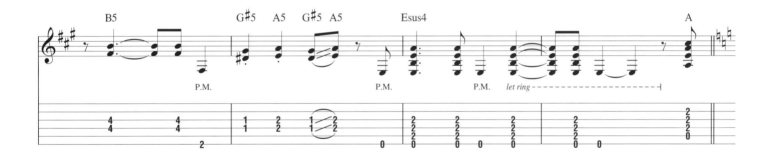

℅ Interlude
w/ classroom noise

Spoken: Hey, I heard you missed us, we're back!
Spoken: Ah, man, I think the clock is

*Switch to neck pickup, w/ vol. control set to 1/2 vol.

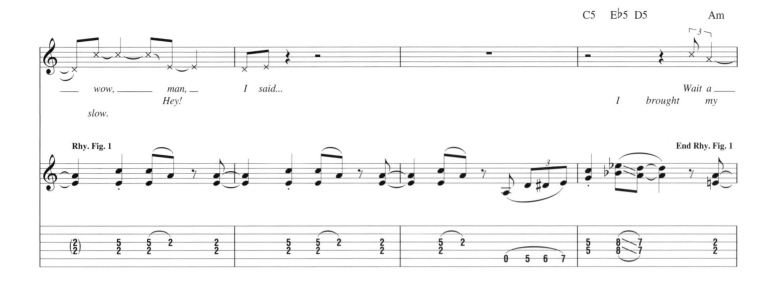

_____ wow, _____ man, _____ I said...
Hey!
slow.

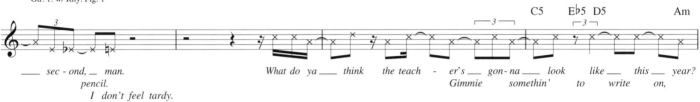

_____ sec - ond, _____ man.
   pencil.
    I don't feel tardy.

What do ya _____ think the teach - er's _____ gon- na _____ look like _____ this _____ year?
Gimmie somethin' to write on,

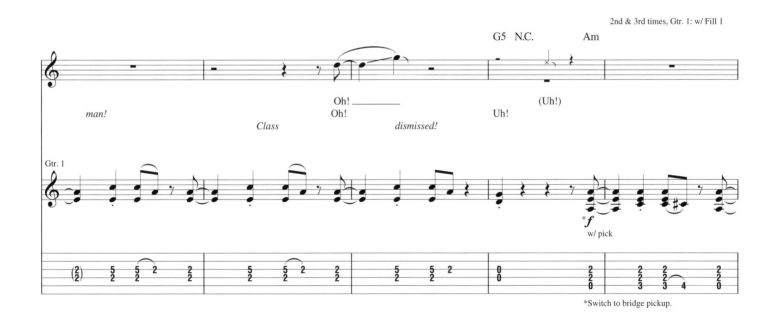

man!
   Class

Oh! _____
Oh! dismissed!

(Uh!)
Uh!

*Switch to bridge pickup.

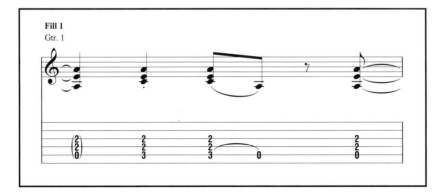

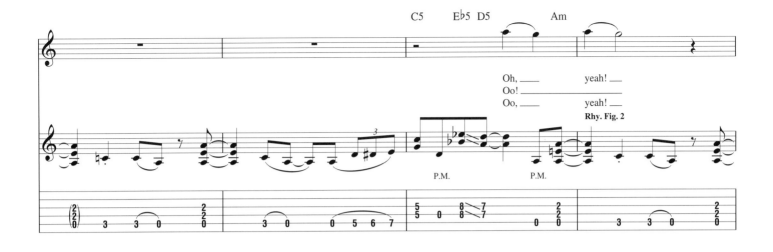

Oh, _____ yeah! _____
Oo! _____
Oo, _____ yeah! ?

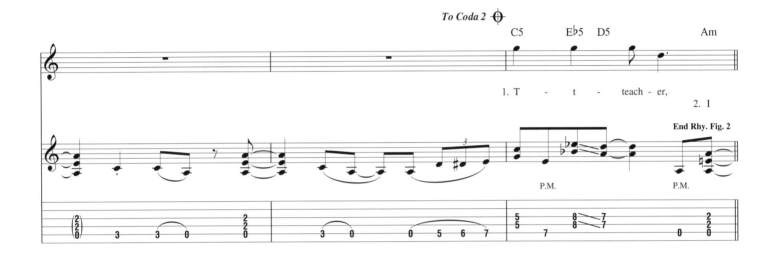

To Coda 2 ⊕

1. T - t - t - teach - er,
2. I

Verse
Gtr. 1: w/ Rhy. Fig. 2 (3 times)

stop   that ___ scream - in'. _____   Teach - er, don't you _____ see? _____
heard a - bout ___ your les - sons _____ but   les - sons are   so _____ cold. _____

Don't wan - na   be _____ no   up - town ___ fool. _____
         I _____ know a - bout ___ this ___ school. _____   Lit -

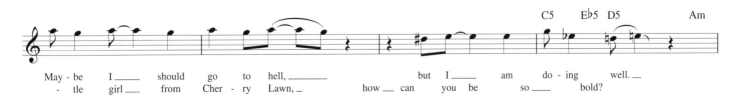

May - be I _____ should   go   to   hell, _____   but I _____ am   do - ing   well. _____
- tle   girl ___ from Cher - ry   Lawn,   how ___ can   you   be   so _____ bold?

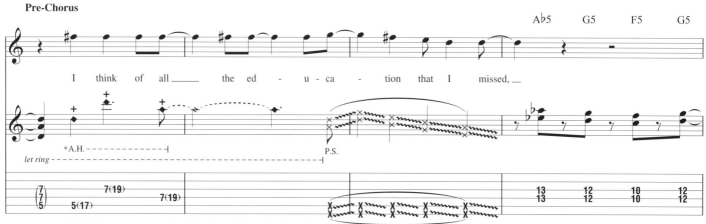

*Artificial harmonics produced by tapping strings 12 frets above fretted notes.

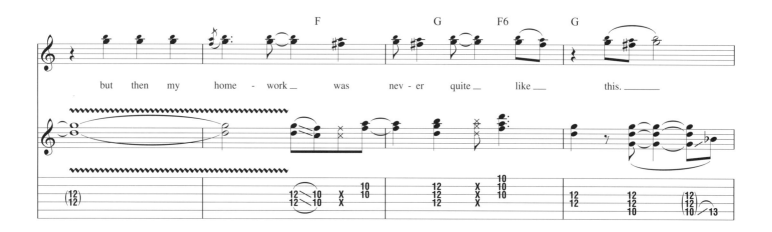

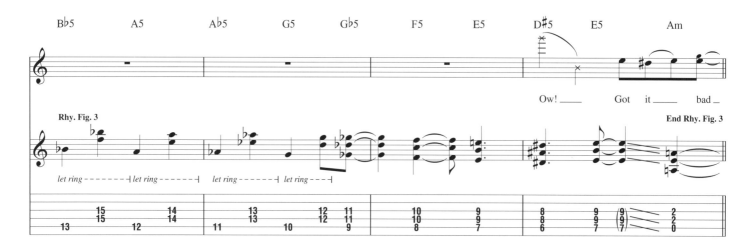

Chorus
Gtr. 1: w/ Rhy. Fig. 2 (3 times)

got it bad, ___ got it bad. ___ I'm hot for teach - er. ___

I've got it bad, ___ so ___ bad. ___ I'm hot for teach -

D.S. al Coda 1

- er. ___

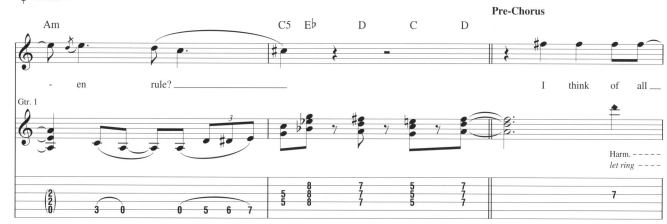

⊕ Coda 1

Pre-Chorus

- en rule? _____ I think of all ___

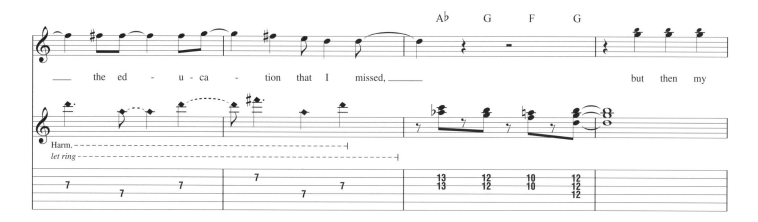

___ the ed - u - ca - tion that I missed, ___ but then my

home-work __ was __ nev-er quite __ like __ this. __

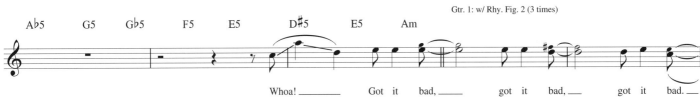

Chorus
Gtr. 1: w/ Rhy. Fig. 2 (3 times)

Whoa! __ Got it bad, __ got it bad, __ got it bad. __

I'm hot for teach - er. __

I've got it bad, __ so bad. __ I'm hot for teach -

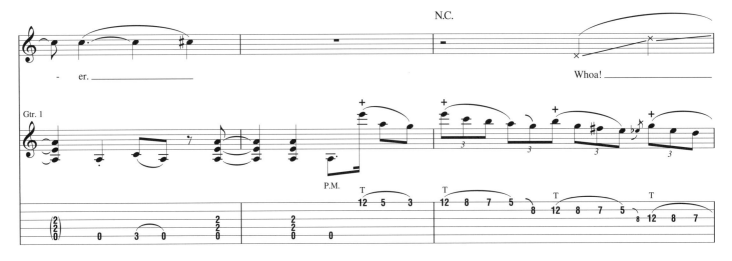

- er. __ Whoa! __

Guitar Solo

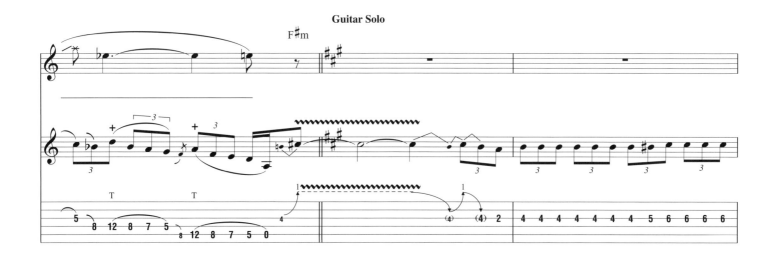

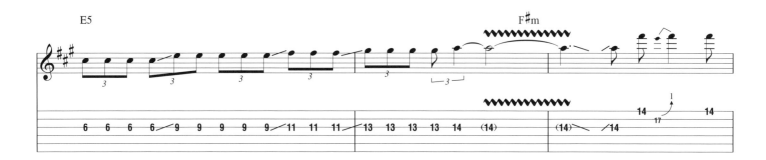

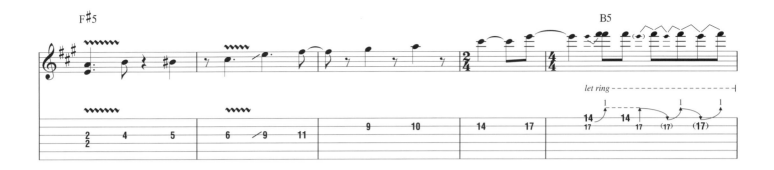

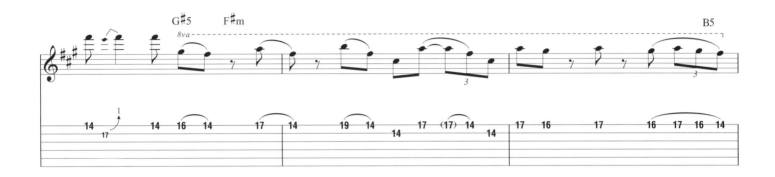

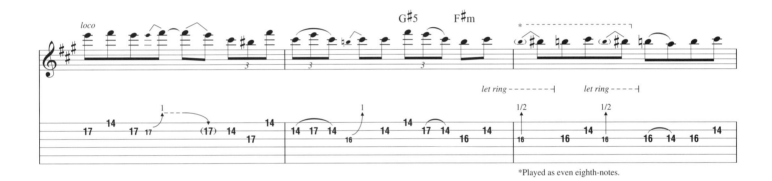

*Played as even eighth-notes.

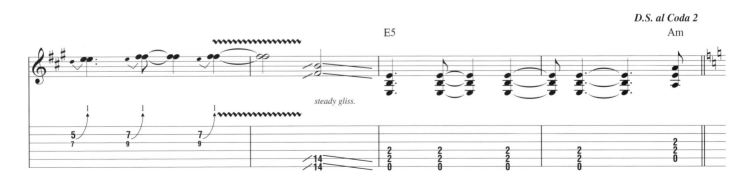

48

Chorus

I've got it bad, ____ got it bad, got it bad. ____

I'm hot for teach - er. ____ Oh!

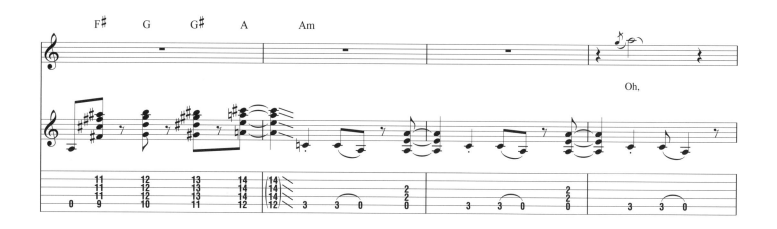

Oh,

yes ____ I'm hot! ____ Wow! _____

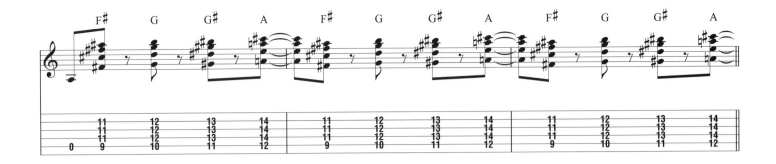

Outro
Free time

Spoken: Oh, _____ my _____ God!

Whoo!

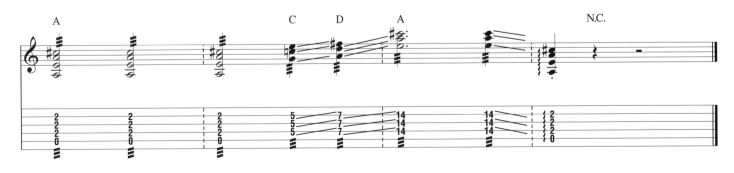

I Can't Quit You Baby

Written by Willie Dixon

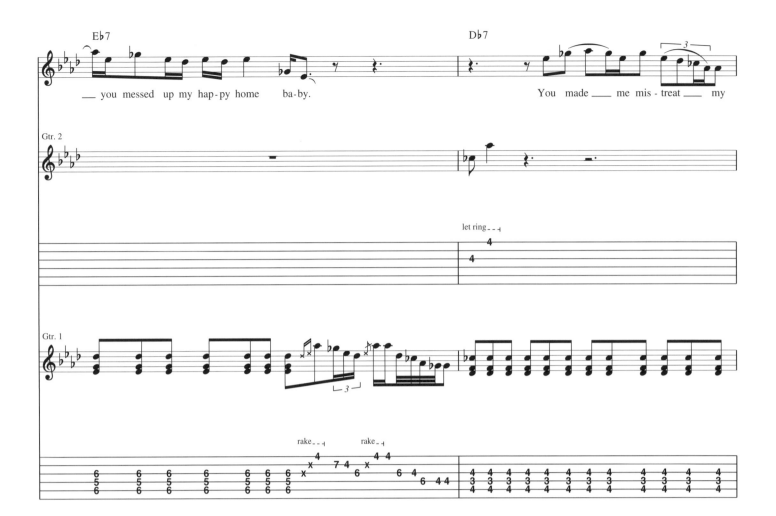

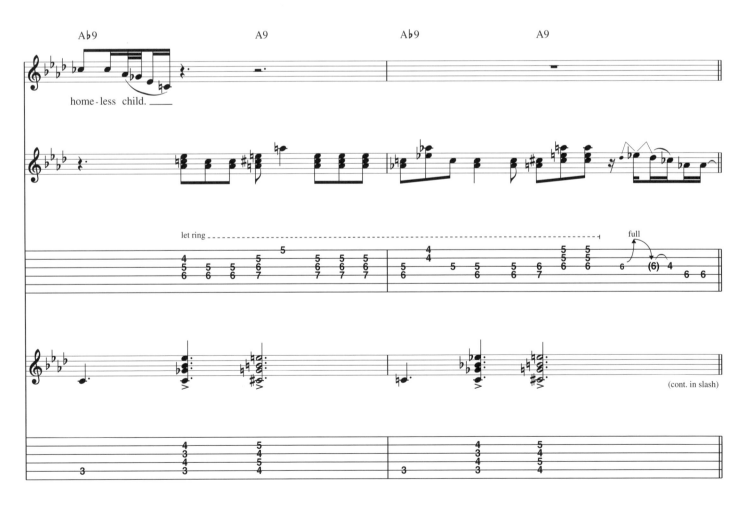

Verse

2. Yes,__ you know I love__ you, babe.

My love for you ___ I could nev-er hide. ___

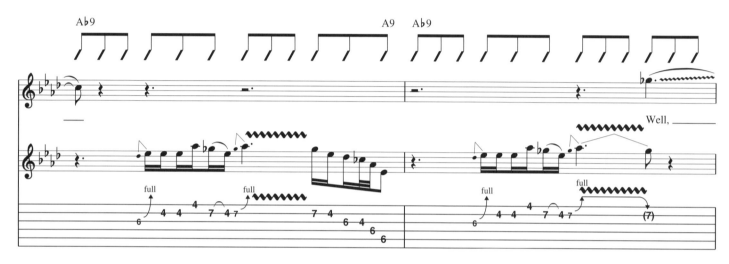

Well, _____

you know__ I love you, babe. _____

My__ love__for you _____ I could nev-er hide.__

(cont. in notation)

Yes, you know

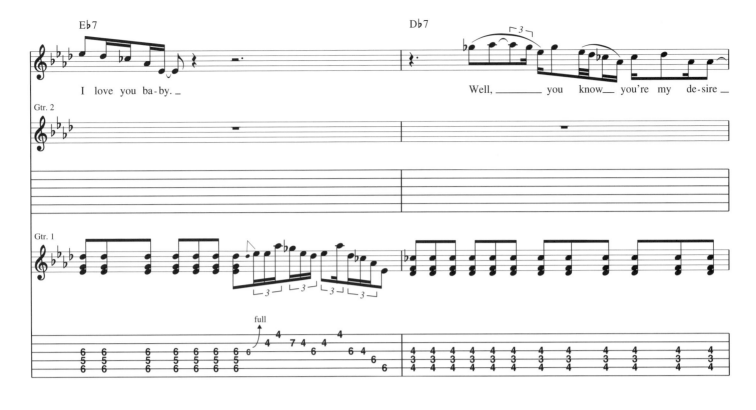

I love you ba-by.

Well,_____ you know__ you're my de-sire__

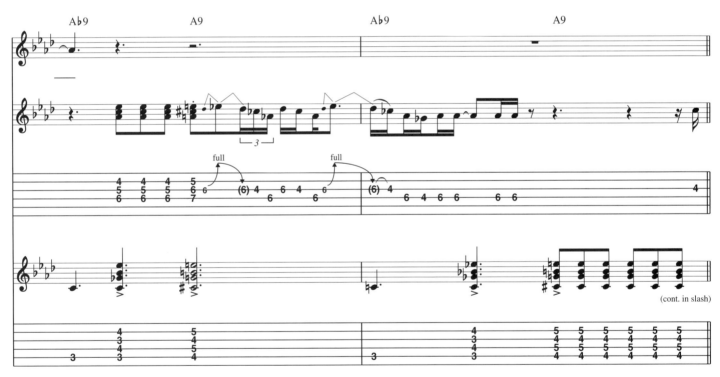

(cont. in slash)

Guitar Solo

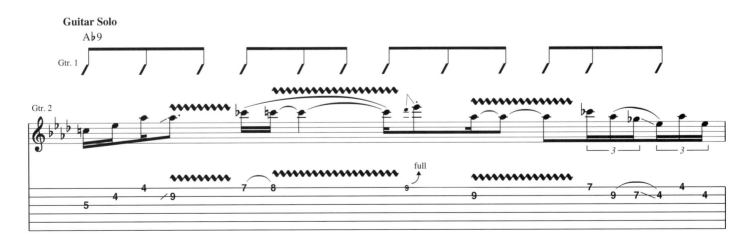

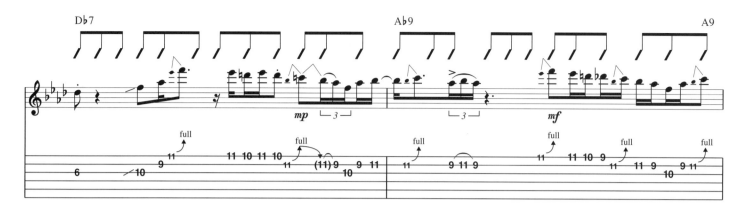

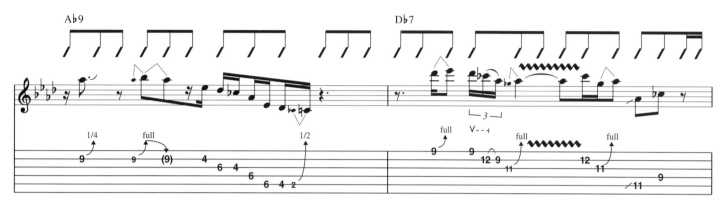

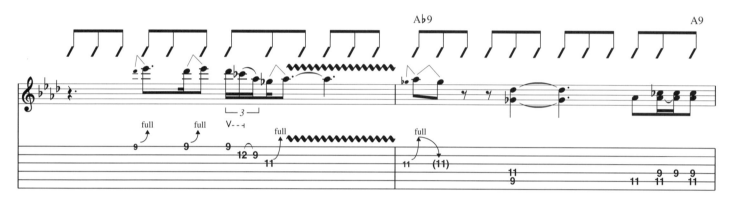

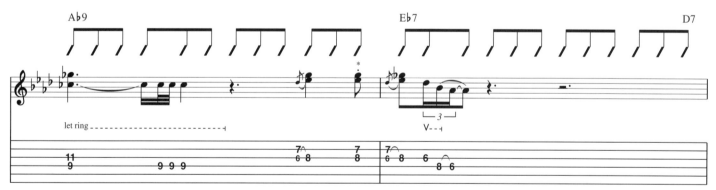

* Only lower note is played staccato.

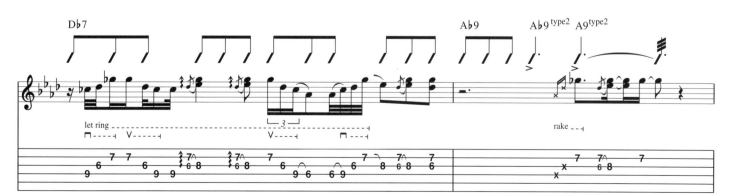

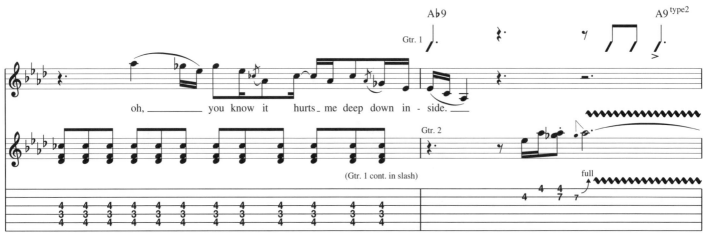

Yes,   when you hear me hol-ler, ba-by,

well, _____ you know ___ you're my   de-sire. ___

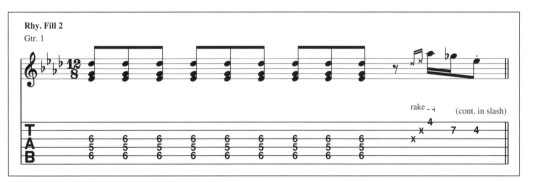

Pour Some Sugar on Me

Words and Music by Joe Elliott, Phil Collen, Richard Savage, Richard Allen, Steve Clark and Robert Lange

*Chord symbols reflect implied harmony.

**Vol. swell

***Vol. swell

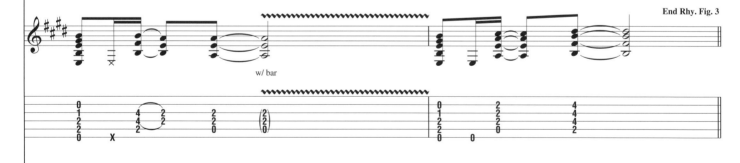

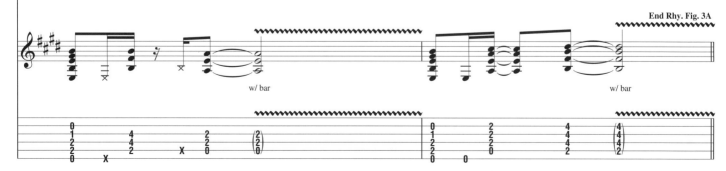

Chorus

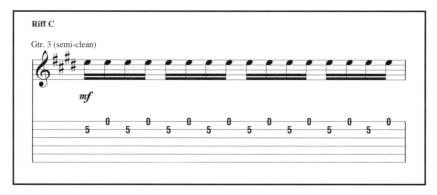

Interlude

Gtr. 1: w/ Riff A
Bkgd. Voc.: w/ Voc. Fig. 1 (3 times)

Verse

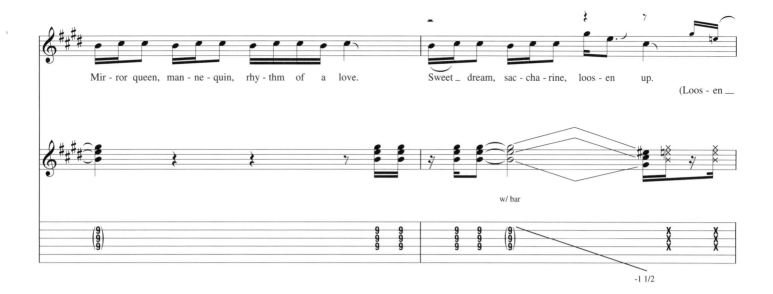

Mir - ror queen, man - ne - quin, rhy - thm of a love. Sweet _ dream, sac - cha - rine, loos - en up. (Loos - en _

w/ bar

-1 1/2

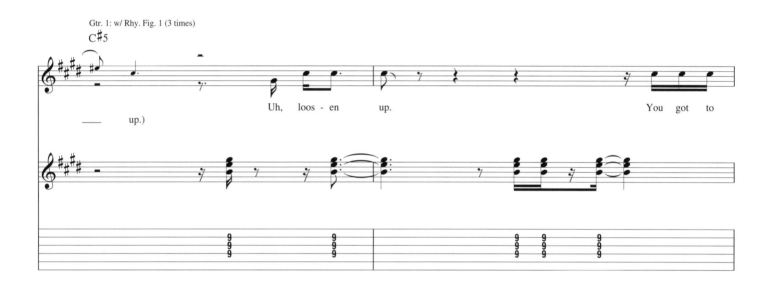

Gtr. 1: w/ Rhy. Fig. 1 (3 times)

C#5

_ up.) Uh, loos - en up. You got to

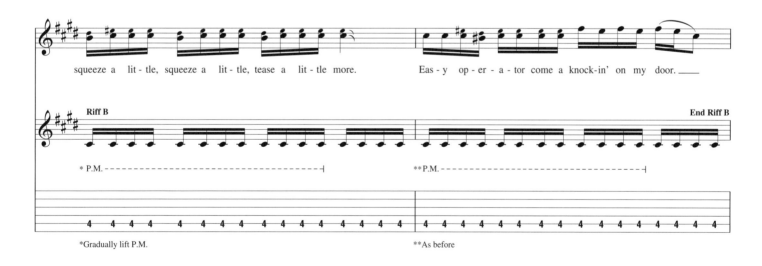

squeeze a lit - tle, squeeze a lit - tle, tease a lit - tle more. Eas - y op - er - a - tor come a knock-in' on my door. _

Riff B

End Riff B

* P.M. - ⌐ **P.M. - ⌐

*Gradually lift P.M. **As before

Gtr. 2: w/ Riff B

Some - time, an - y - time, sug - ar me sweet. Lit - tle miss in - no - cent sug - ar me. Yeah. _

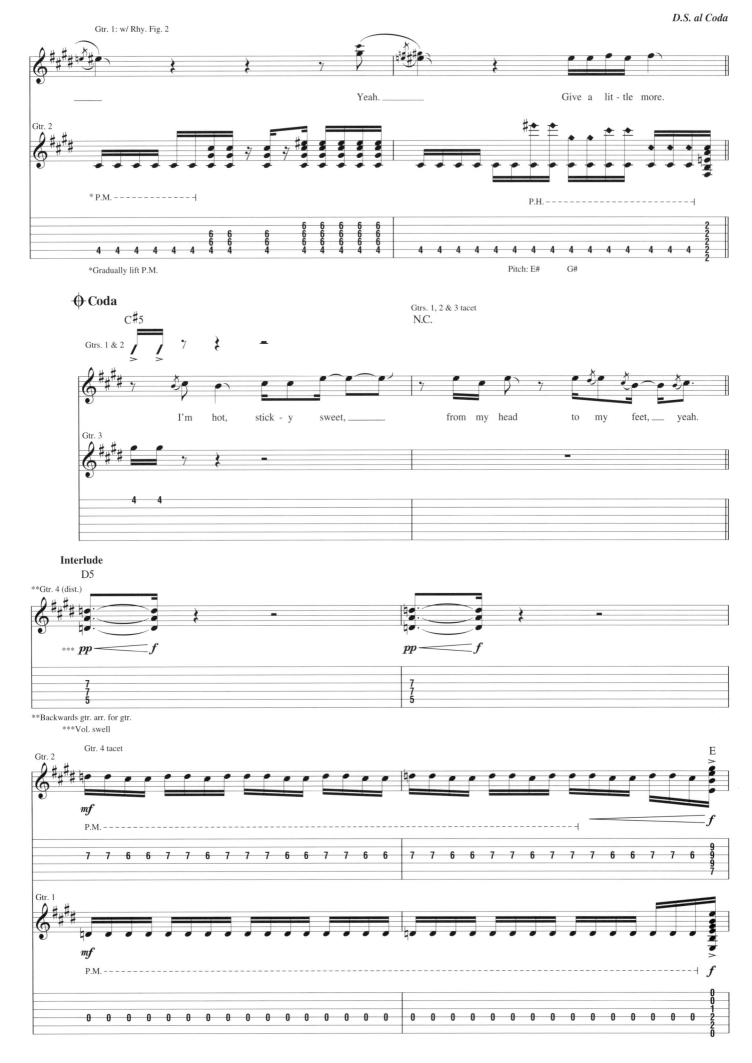

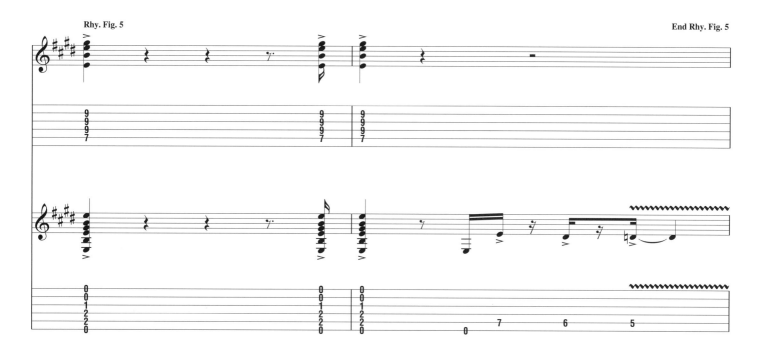

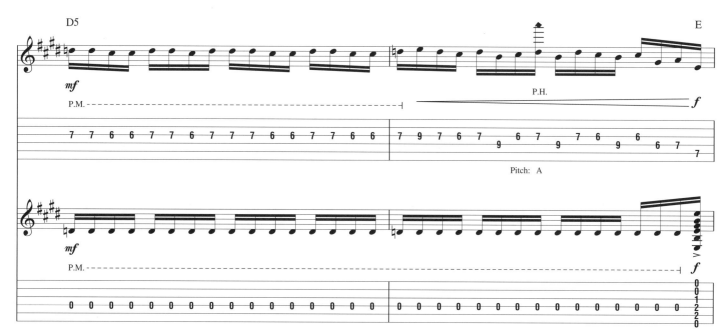

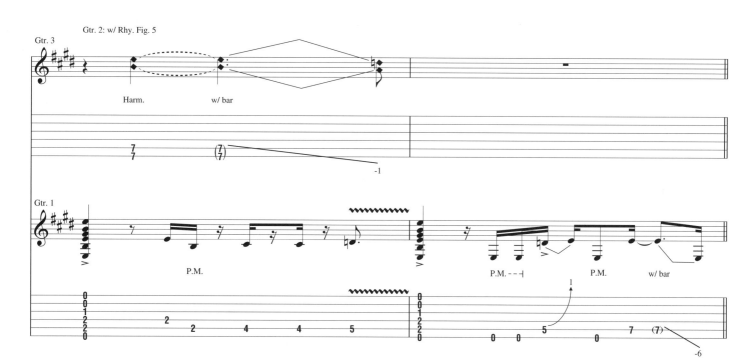

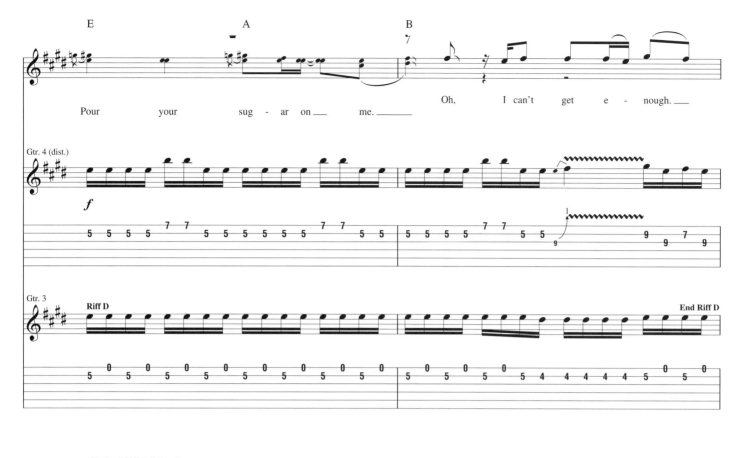

Pour your sug - ar on ____ me. ____

Oh, I can't get e - nough. ____

Pour some sug - ar on ____ me. ____

Oh, in the name of love. ____

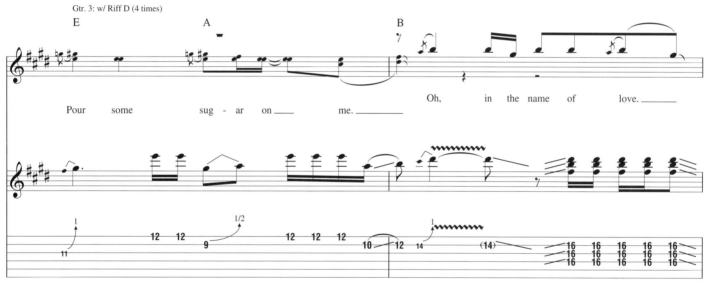

Pour some sug - ar on ____ me. ____

Get it, come get it.

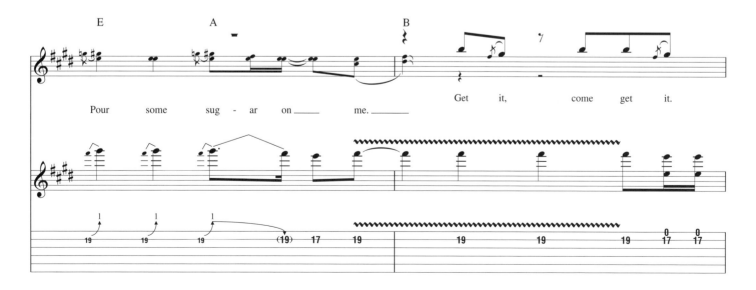

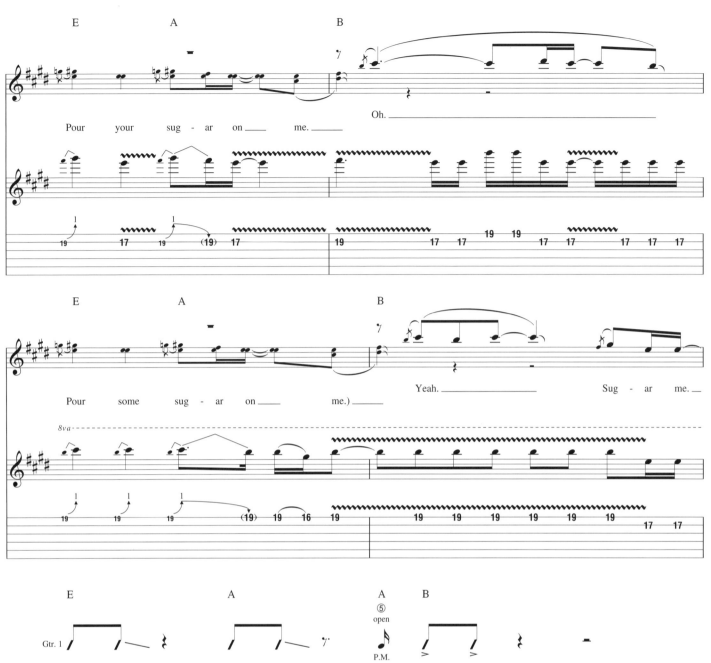

Pour your sug - ar on ____ me. ____

Oh. ____

Pour some sug - ar on ____ me.) ____

Yeah. ____ Sug - ar me. ____

Revolution

Words and Music by John Lennon and Paul McCartney

† All Gtrs: Capo II

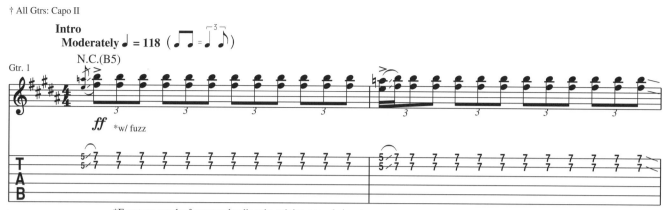

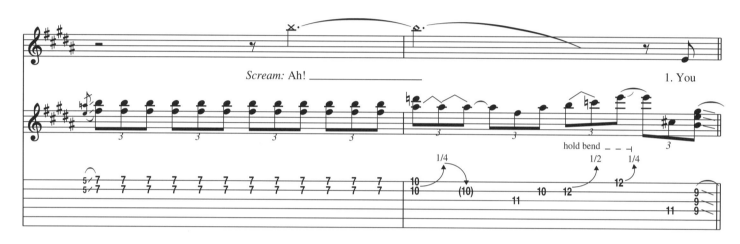

*Fuzztone results from overloading the mixing console input.
†Notes tabbed at 2nd fret played as open strings.

*Tie 1st time only.

we all want _ to change the world.   You
we'd all love _ to see the plan.   You
we all want _ to change your head.   You

tell me that it's ev - o - lu - tion,_____ well,_____ you know,__
ask me for a con - tri - bu - tion,_____ well,_____ you know,__
tell me it's the in - sti - tu - tion,_____ well,_____ you know,__

we all want __ to change the world. _____
we are do - in' what we can. _____
you bet - ter free your mind in - stead. _____

Pre - Chorus

But when you talk a - bout de - struc - tion, _____
But if you want money for people with minds that hate, _____
But if you go car - ry - in' pic - tures of Chair - man Mao, _____

don't you know that you can count me out? _____
all I can tell you is broth- er, you have to wait. _____
ya ain't gonna make it with any - one an - y - how. _____

*Play C♯5/G♯ 1st time only.
 Add parenthesized notes on 2nd & 3rd verses.

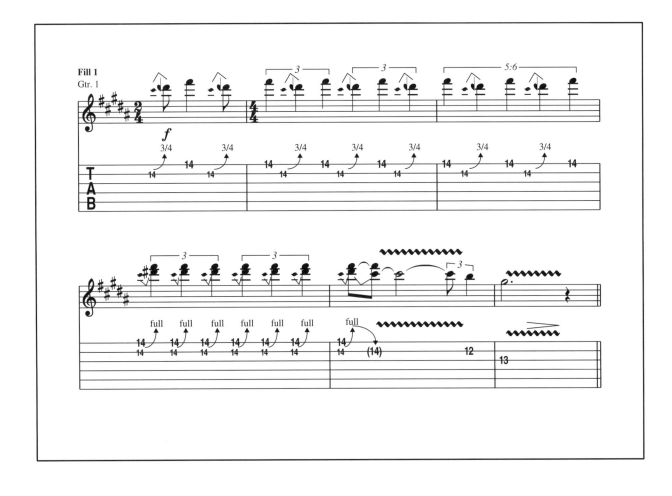

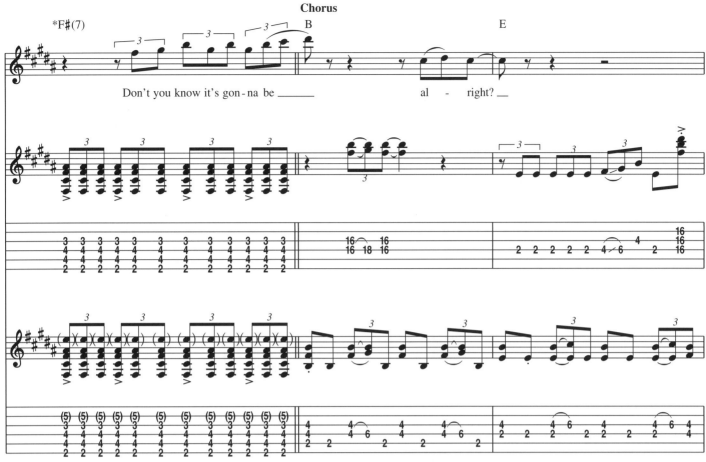

Chorus

Don't you know it's gon-na be _____ al - right? ____

*Add E in parens. (7th) on D.S. only.

Al - right. ____ Al - right. ____

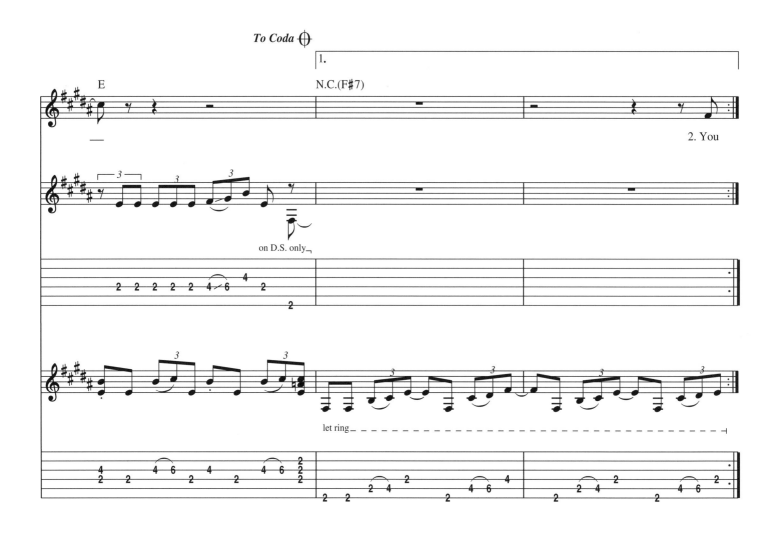

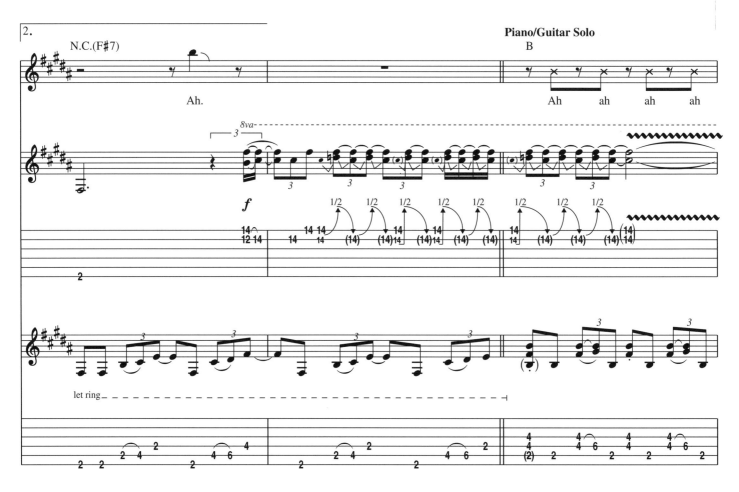

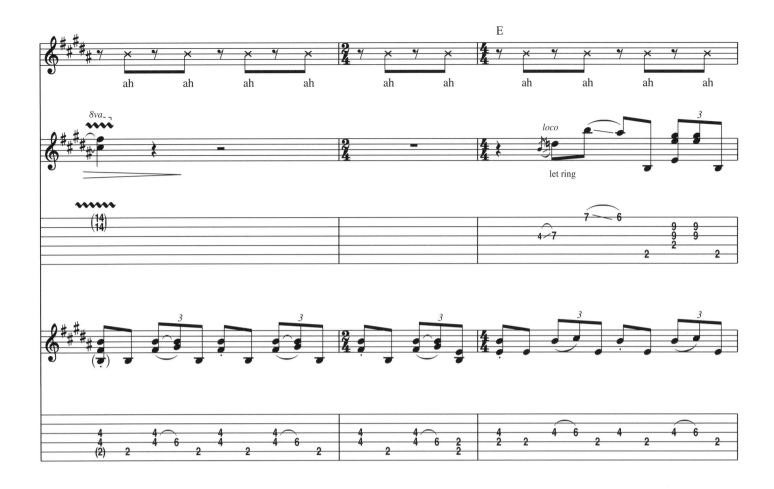

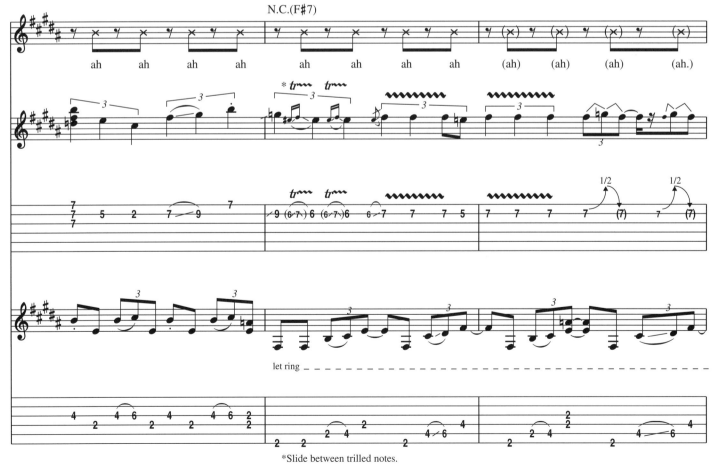

*Slide between trilled notes.

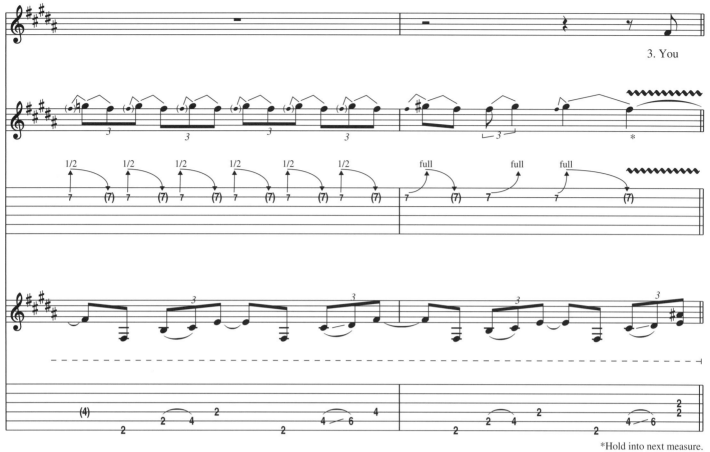

3. You

*Hold into next measure.

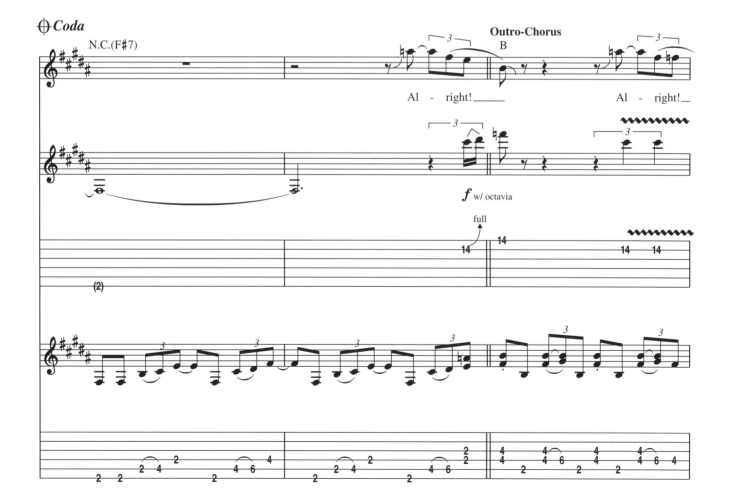

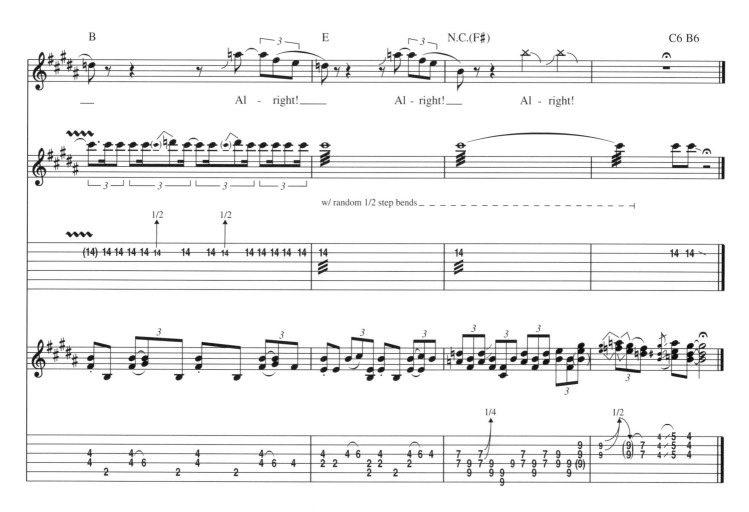

Bennie and the Jets

Words and Music by Elton John and Bernie Taupin

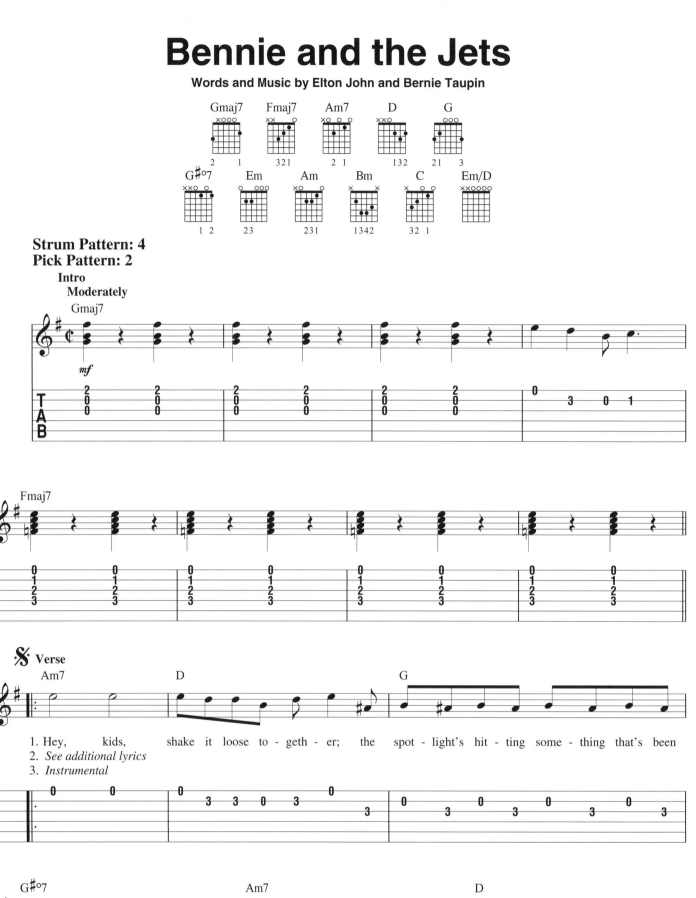

Strum Pattern: 4
Pick Pattern: 2

Intro
Moderately

1. Hey, kids, shake it loose to-geth-er; the spot-light's hit-ting some-thing that's been
2. *See additional lyrics*
3. *Instrumental*

known to change the weath-er. We'll kill the fat-ted calf to-night, so stick a-

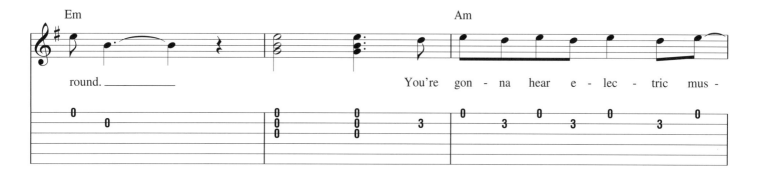

round._____ You're gon - na hear e - lec - tric mus -

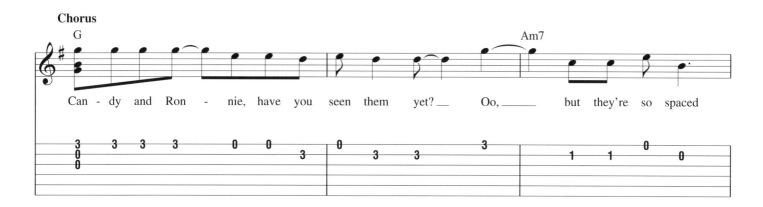

\- ic, sol - id walls of sound. _____ Say,

3rd time, Instrumental ends

Chorus

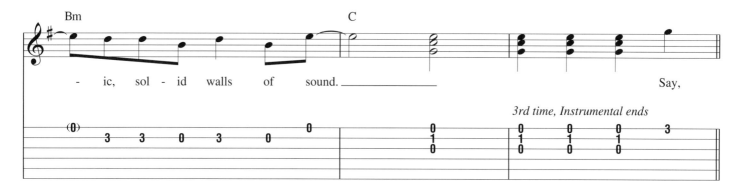

Can - dy and Ron - nie, have you seen them yet? _ Oo, _____ but they're so spaced

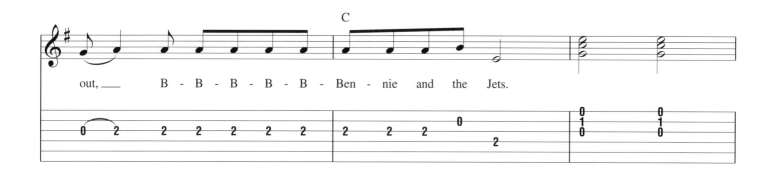

out, _ B - B - B - B - B - Ben - nie and the Jets.

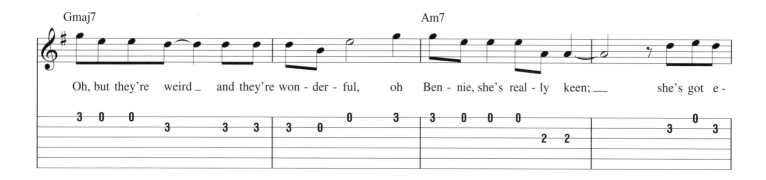

Oh, but they're weird _ and they're won - der - ful, oh Ben - nie, she's real - ly keen; _ she's got e -

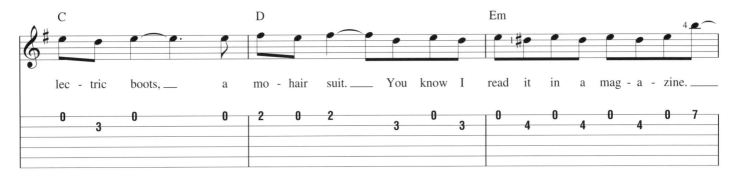

C   D   Em

lec - tric boots, ___ a mo - hair suit. ___ You know I read it in a mag - a - zine. ___

To Coda ⊕

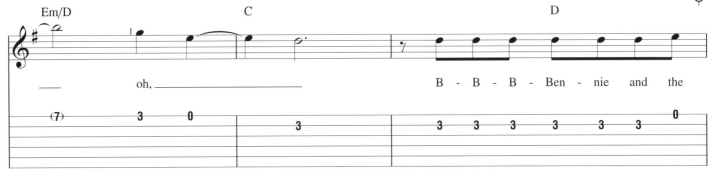

Em/D   C   D

___ oh, ___ B - B - B - Ben - nie and the

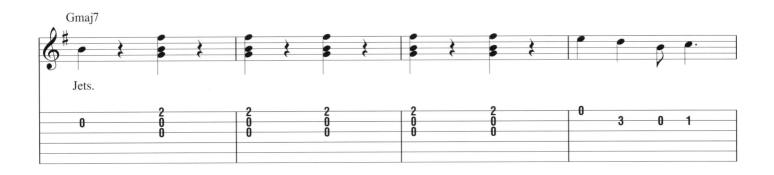

Gmaj7

Jets.

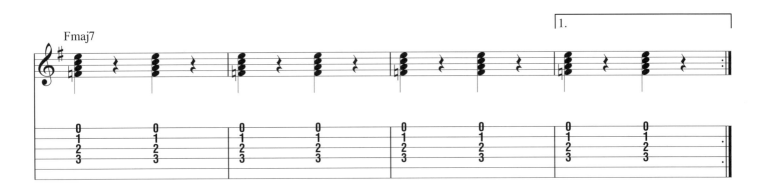

Fmaj7   1.

⊕ **Coda**

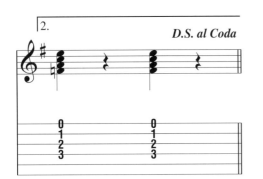

2.

D.S. al Coda

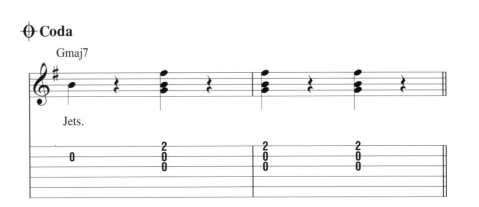

Gmaj7

Jets.

Outro

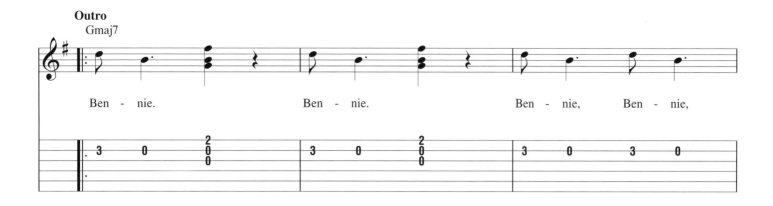

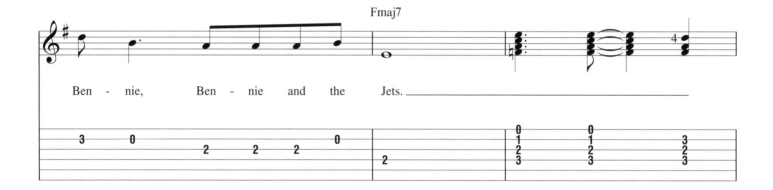

Repeat and fade

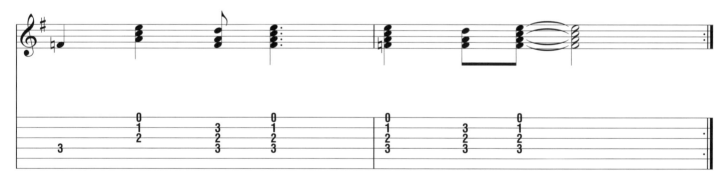

Additional Lyrics

2. Hey, kids, plug into the faithless,
   Maybe they're blinded, but Bennie makes them ageless.
   We shall survive; let us take ourselves along
   Where we fight our parents out in the streets
   To find who's right and who's wrong.

Buddy Holly

Words and Music by Rivers Cuomo

Oh, no what do we do? Don't look now but I lost my shoe.

I can't run and I can't kick. What's the mat-ter, babe, are you feel-in' sick?

What's a mat-ter, what's a mat-ter, what's a mat-ter you? What's a mat-ter, babe, are you feel-in' blue?

C   Bm   Em
Oh, _____ oh, oh, oh, oh, oh, oh. _____

D.S. al Coda

C   Cm
(And that's for all _____

84

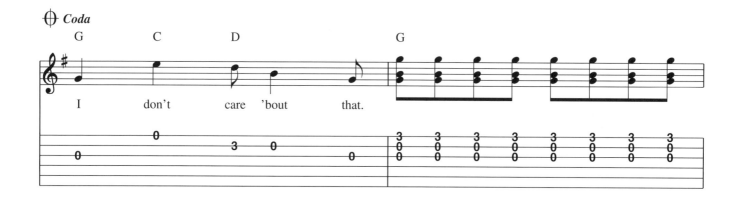

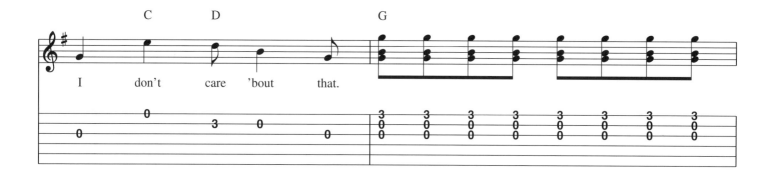

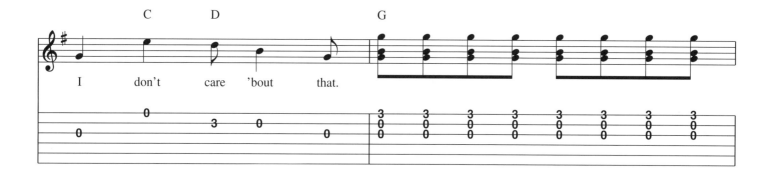

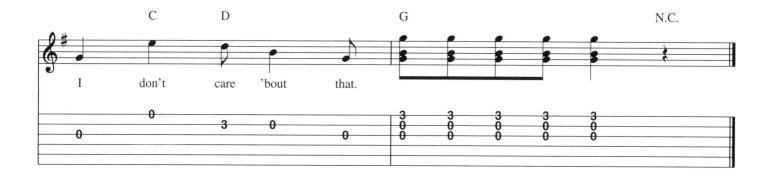

Additional Lyrics

2. Don't you ever fear, I'm always near.
   I know that you need help.
   Your tongue is twisted, your eyes are slit.
   You need a guardian.

Bye Bye Bye

Words and Music by Kristian Lundin, Jake Carlsson and Andreas Carlsson

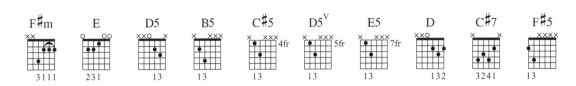

*Capo II

Strum Pattern: 2, 3
Pick Pattern: 3, 4

Intro
Moderately slow

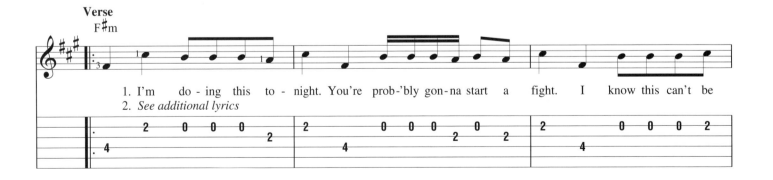

*Optional: To match recording, place capo at 2nd fret.

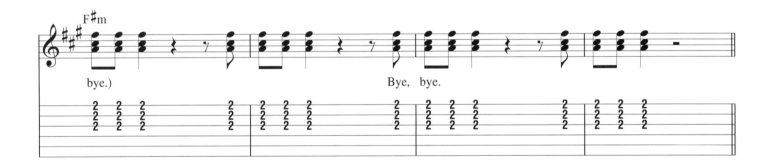

bye.)   Bye,   bye.

Verse

1. I'm do-ing this to-night. You're prob-'bly gon-na start a fight. I know this can't be
2. *See additional lyrics*

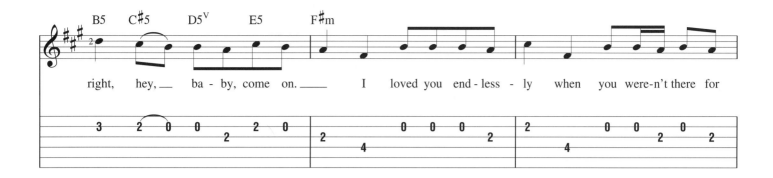

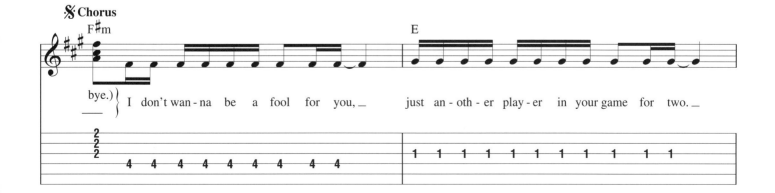

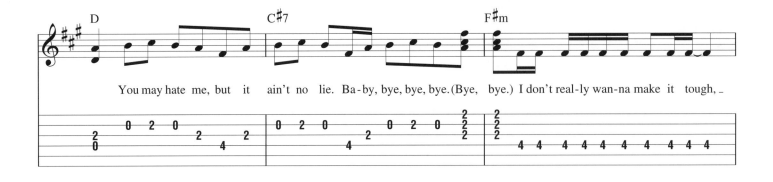

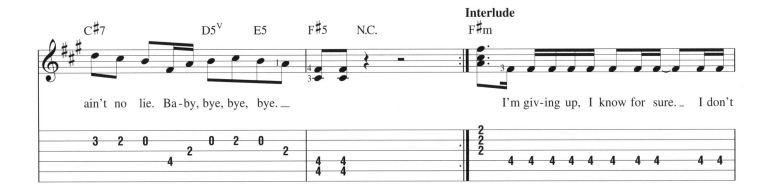

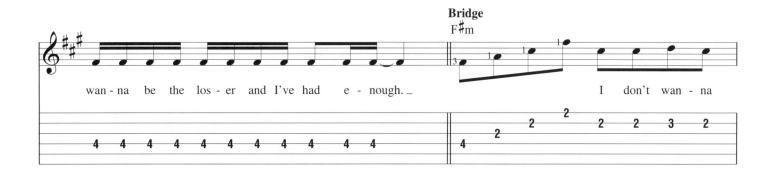

Bridge

wan - na be the los - er and I've had e - nough. ___   I don't wan - na

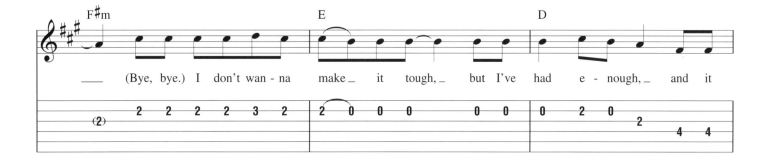

be ___ your fool ___ in this game for two, ___ so I'm leav - ing you be - hind. ___

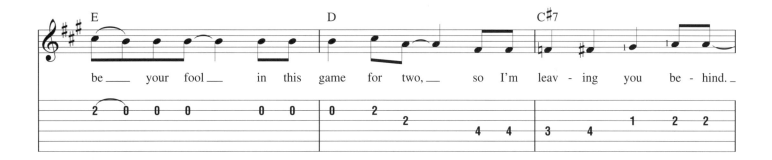

___ (Bye, bye.) I don't wan - na make ___ it tough, ___ but I've had e - nough, ___ and it

✛ **Coda**

D.S. al Coda

ain't no lie. (Bye, bye.) ___   ain't no lie.   Bye, bye, bye. (Bye, bye.)

*Tie into beat one on D.S.

Additional Lyrics

2. Just hit me with truth.
   Now, girl, you're more than welcome to.
   So give me one good reason, baby, come on.
   I live for you and me
   And now I really come to see
   That life would be much better once you're gone.

A Day in the Life

Words and Music by John Lennon and Paul McCartney

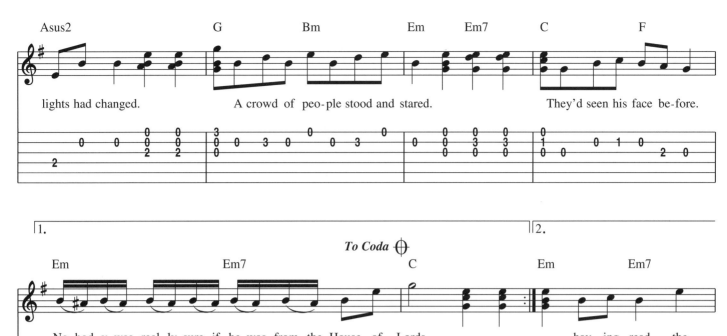

lights had changed.   A crowd of peo-ple stood and stared.   They'd seen his face be-fore.

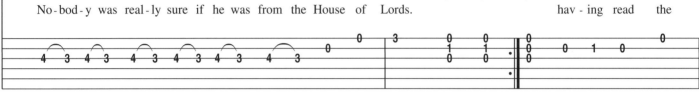

No-bod-y was real-ly sure if he was from the House of Lords.   hav-ing read the

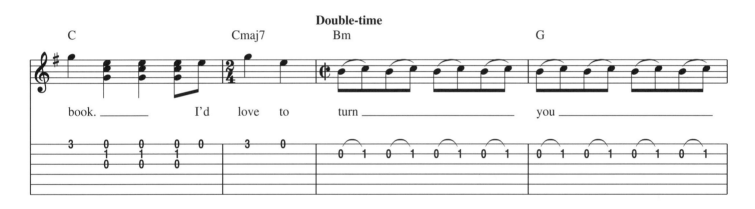

book. _____ I'd love to turn _____ you _____

on. _____

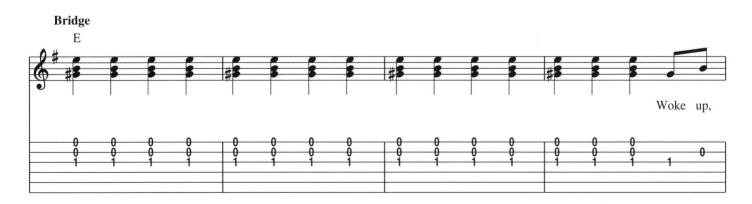

Woke up,

End double-time

Interlude

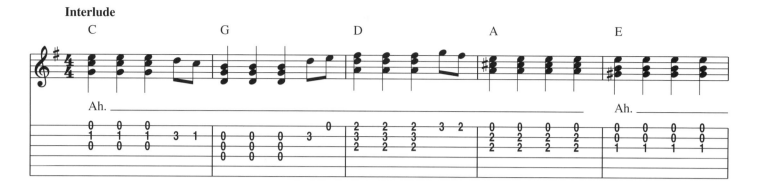

D.S. al Coda
(take 1st ending)

⊕ **Coda**

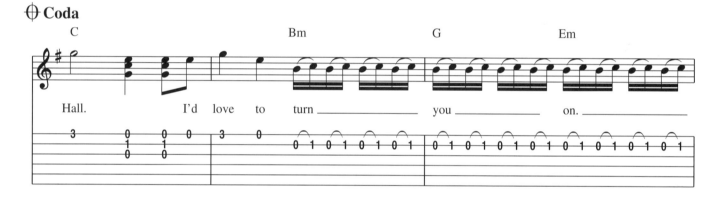

Additional Lyrics

3. I saw a film today, oh boy.
   The English army had just won the war.
   A crowd of people turned away.
   But, I just had to look,
   Having read the book.
   I'd love to turn you on.

4. I read the news today, oh boy.
   Four thousands holes in Blackburn, Lancashire.
   And though the holes were rather small,
   They had to count them all.
   Now they know how many holes
   It takes to fill the Albert Hall.
   I'd love to turn you on.

Faith

Words and Music by George Michael

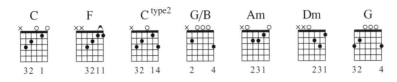

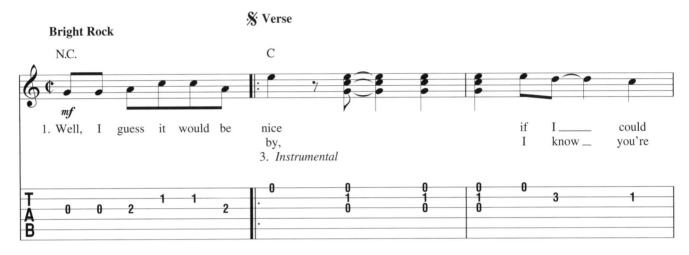

Strum Pattern: 6
Pick Pattern: 6

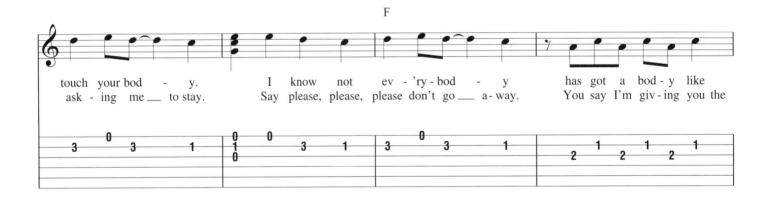

give my heart __ a - way.　　And I know all the games __ you play　　be - cause I play them
ev - 'ry word __ you say.　　Can't help but think of yes - ter - day　　and an - oth - er who

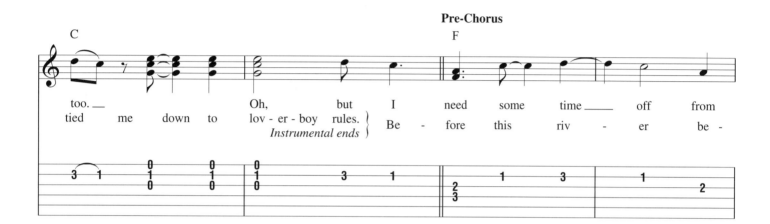

Pre-Chorus

too. __　　Oh,　　but I　　need some time _____ off from
tied me down to lov - er - boy rules. }　　Be - fore this riv - er be -
Instrumental ends }

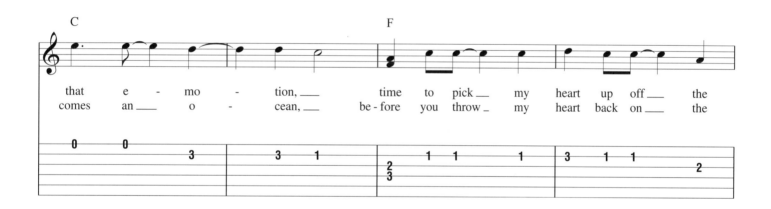

that e - mo - tion, ___　　time to pick __ my heart up off ___ the
comes an ___ o - cean, ___　　be - fore you throw __ my heart back on ___ the

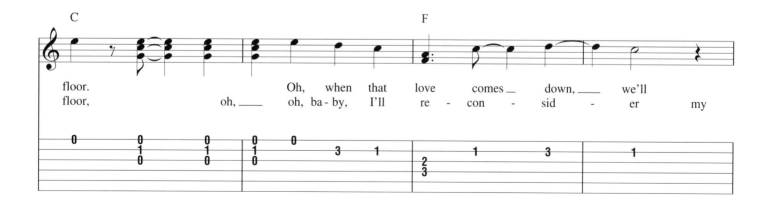

floor.　　Oh, when that love comes __ down, ___ we'll
floor,　　oh, ___ oh, ba - by, I'll re - con - sid - er my

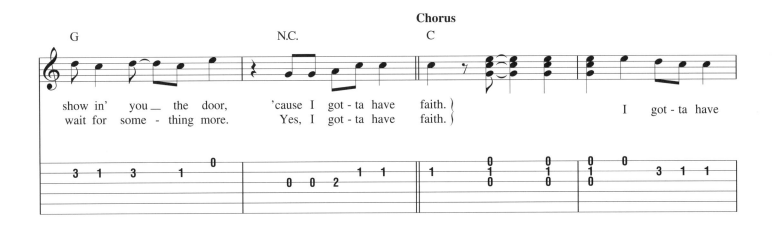

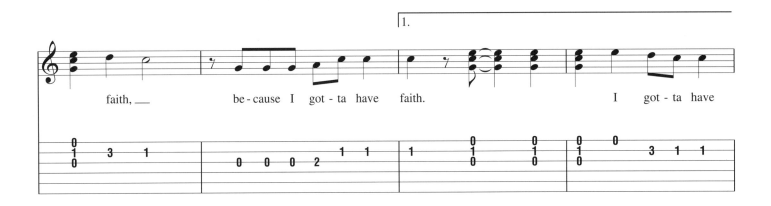

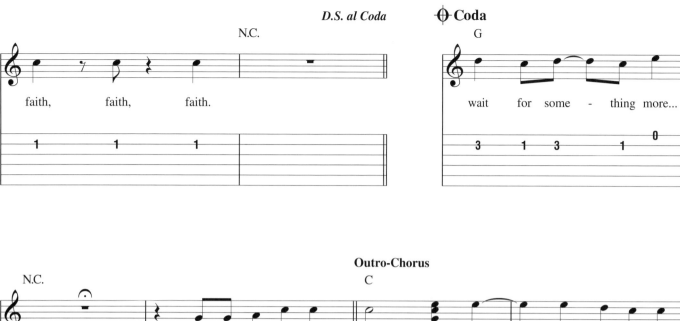

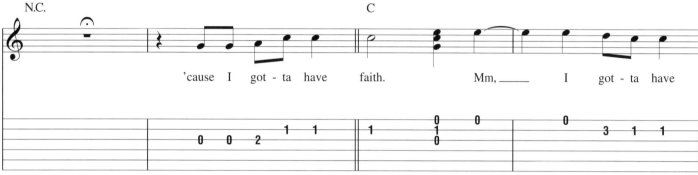

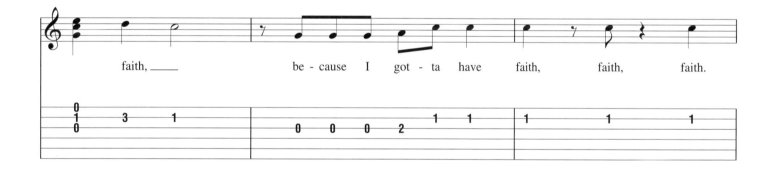

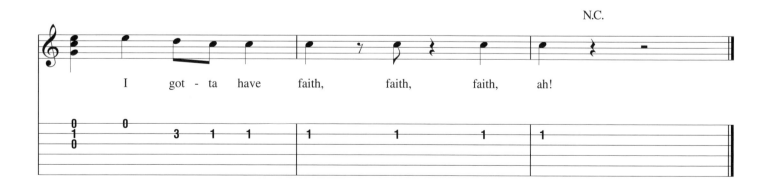

Free Fallin'

Words and Music by Tom Petty and Jeff Lynne

Strum Pattern: 6
Pick Pattern: 6

Intro
Moderate Rock

mf

1. She's a

Verse

good girl, ___ loves her ma - ma, loves Je - sus, ___ and A -

mer - i - ca, too. ___ She's a good girl, ___ cra - zy 'bout El - vis, loves

hor - ses, ___ and her boy - friend, too. ___

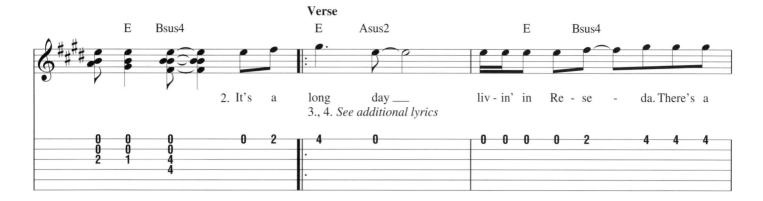

Verse

2. It's a long day ___ liv - in' in Re - se - da. There's a
3., 4. *See additional lyrics*

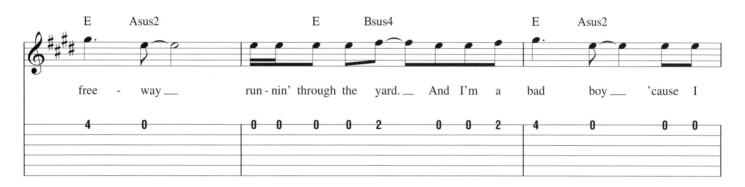

free - way ___ run - nin' through the yard. ___ And I'm a bad boy ___ 'cause I

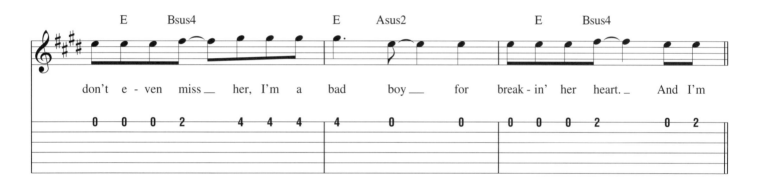

don't e - ven miss ___ her, I'm a bad boy ___ for break - in' her heart. ___ And I'm

Chorus

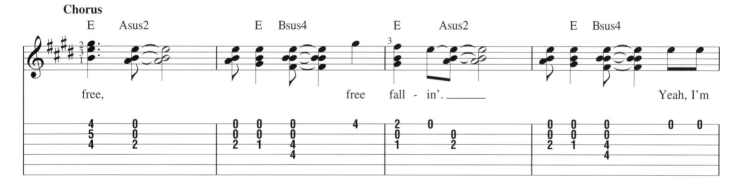

free, free fall - in'. _____ Yeah, I'm

1., 2.

3.

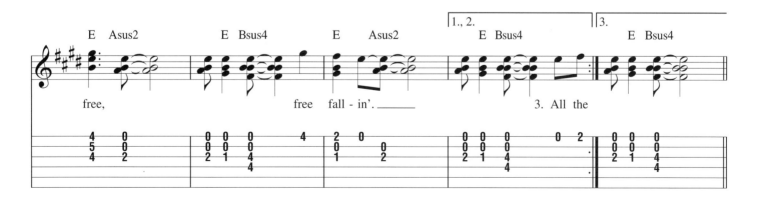

free, free fall - in'. _____ 3. All the

Interlude

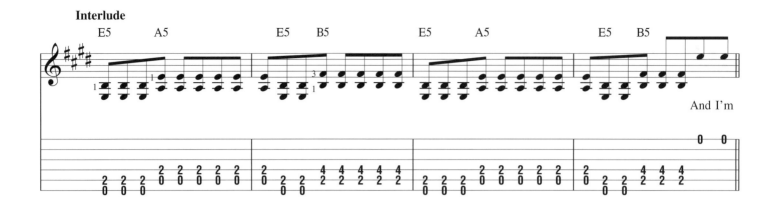

And I'm

Outro-Chorus

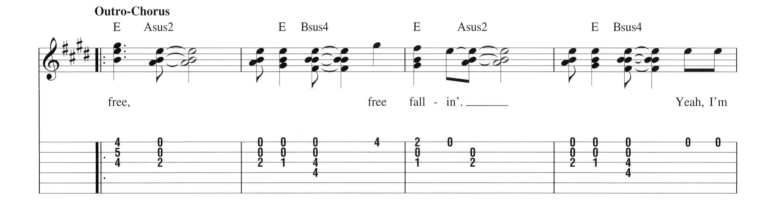

free,   free   fall - in'. _____   Yeah, I'm

Repeat and fade

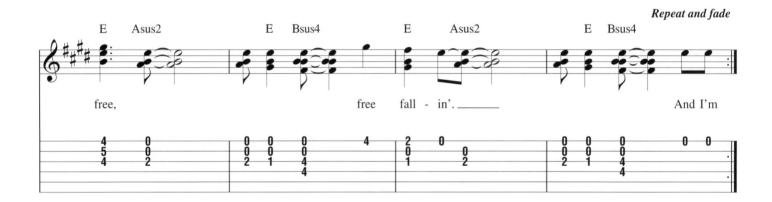

free,   free   fall - in'. _____   And I'm

Additional Lyrics

3. All the vampires walkin' through the valley
   Move west down Ventura Boulevard.
   And all the bad boys are standing in the shadows.
   And the good girls are home with broken hearts.

4. Wanna glide down over Mulholland.
   I wanna write her name in the sky.
   I wanna free fall out into nothin'.
   Gonna leave this world for a while.

Good Times

Words and Music by Nile Rodgers and Bernard Edwards

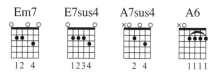

Strum Pattern: 1
Pick Pattern: 3

Intro
Moderately

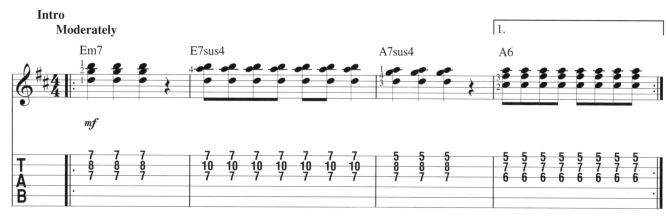

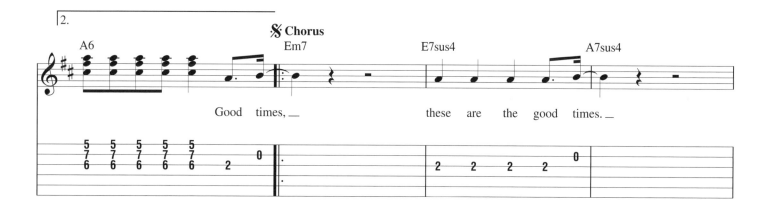

Good times, __ these are the good times. __

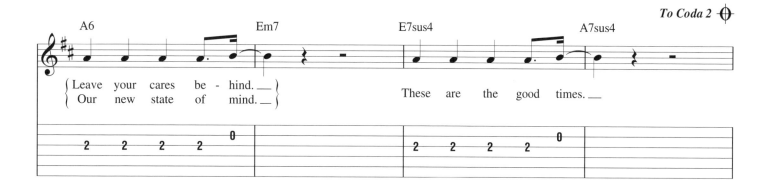

{ Leave your cares be - hind. __ }
{ Our new state of mind. __ }

These are the good times. __

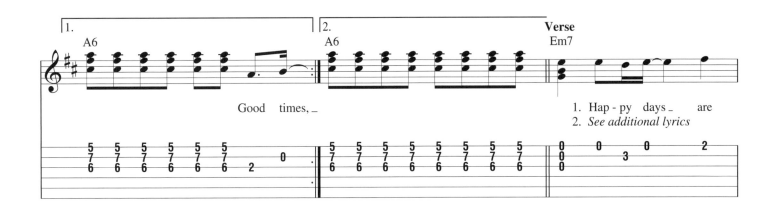

Good times, ___

1. Hap - py days ___ are
2. *See additional lyrics*

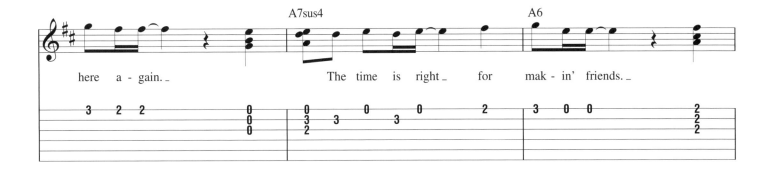

here a - gain. ___ The time is right ___ for mak - in' friends. ___

Let's get to-geth - er. How 'bout a quar - ter to ten? ___ Come to - mor - row, let's

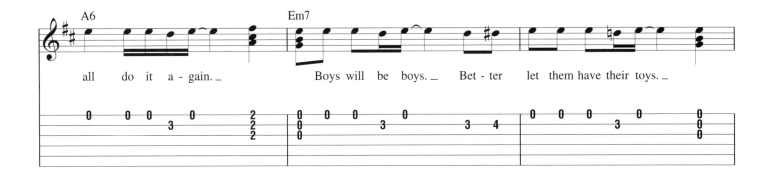

all do it a - gain. ___ Boys will be boys. ___ Bet - ter let them have their toys. ___

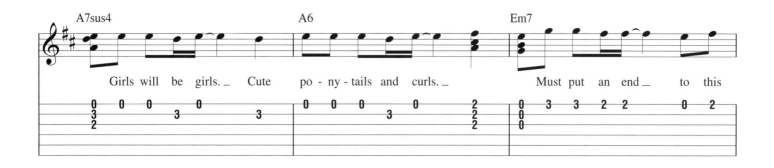

To Coda 1 ⊕

D.S. al Coda 1
(take repeat)

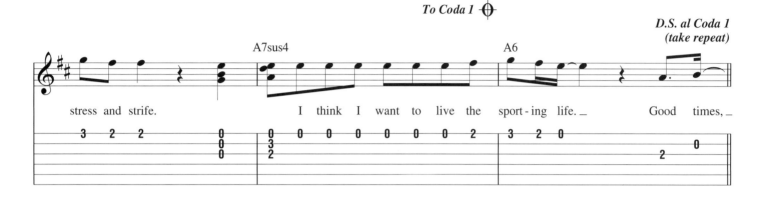

⊕ **Coda 1**

D.S. al Coda 2
(take repeat)

⊕ **Coda 2**

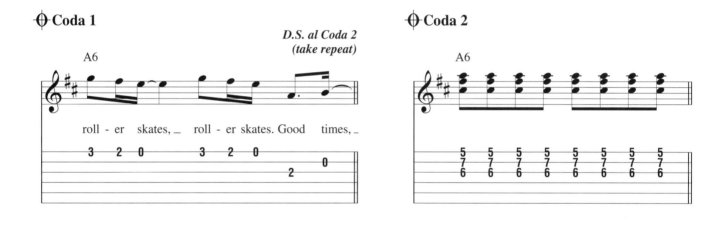

Outro

Repeat and fade

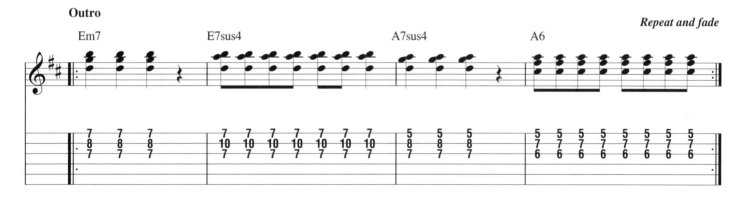

Additional Lyrics

2. A rumor has it that it's getting late.
   Time marches on; just can't wait.
   The clock keeps turnin'. Why hesitate?
   You silly fool, you can't change your fate.
   Let's cut the rug; little jive and jitterbug.
   We want the best. We won't settle for less.
   Don't be a drag. Participate.
   Clams on the half shell and roller skates, roller skates.

Got to Hurry

By Oscar Rasputin

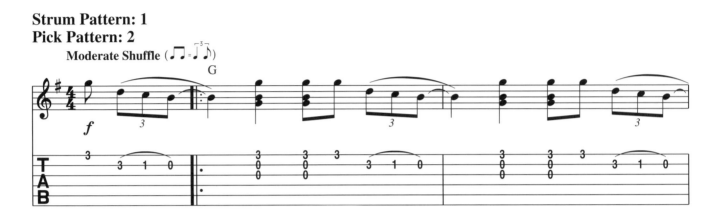

Strum Pattern: 1
Pick Pattern: 2

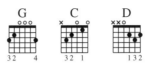

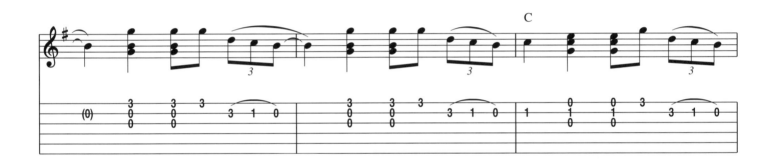

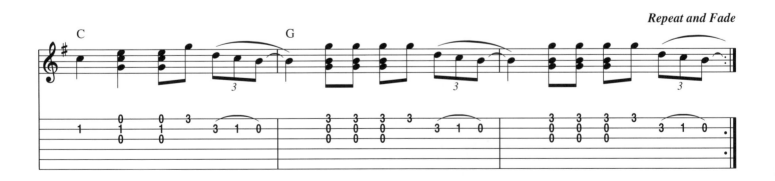

Happy Days

Theme from the Paramount Television Series HAPPY DAYS
Words by Norman Gimbel
Music by Charles Fox

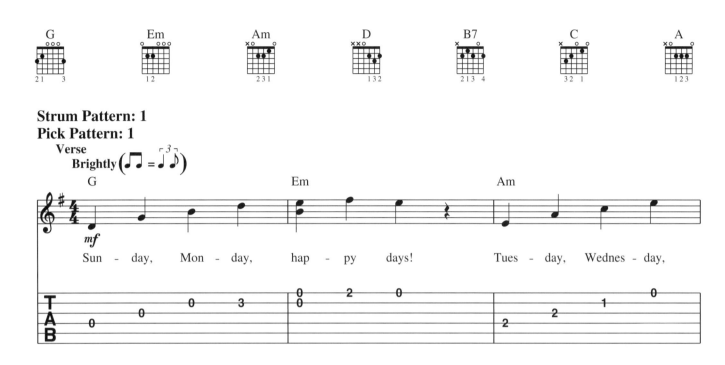

Strum Pattern: 1
Pick Pattern: 1

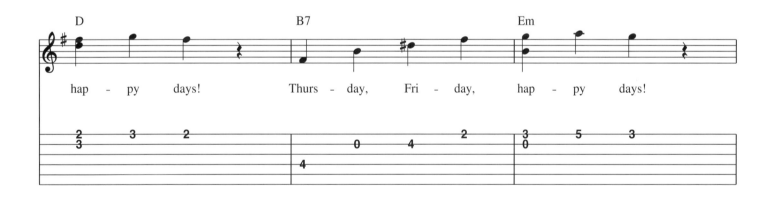

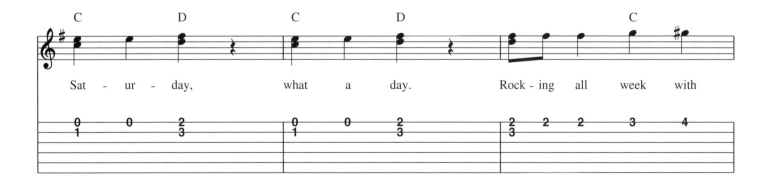

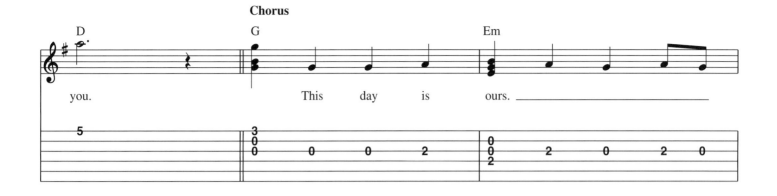

Chorus

you. This day is ours. _____

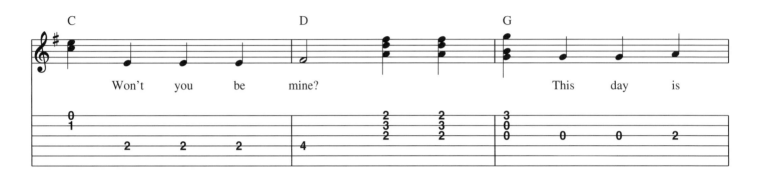

Won't you be mine? This day is

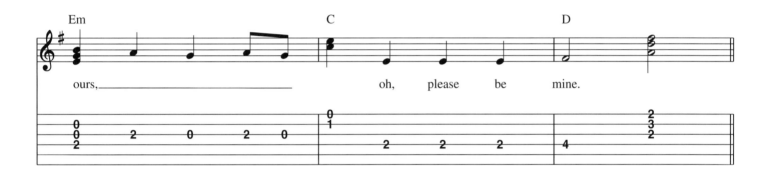

ours, _____ oh, please be mine.

Bridge

Hel - lo, sun - shine, good - bye rain. _____ She's wear - ing my school ring

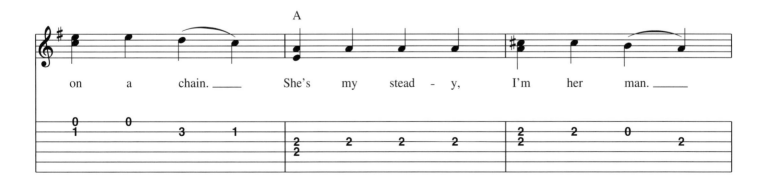

on a chain. _____ She's my stead - y, I'm her man. _____

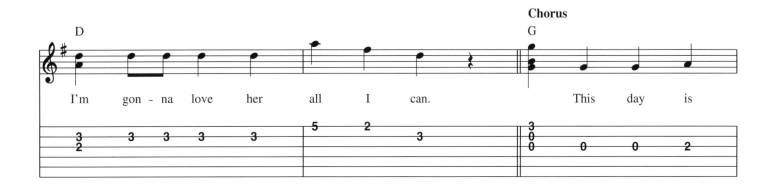

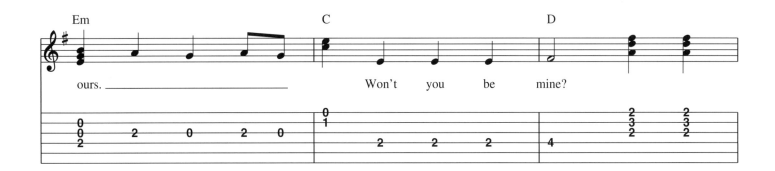

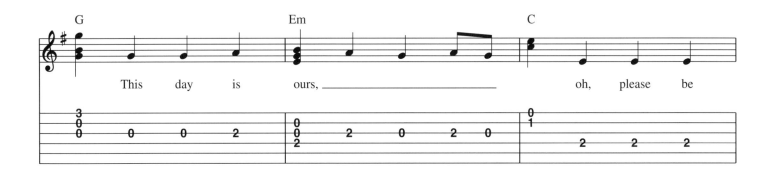

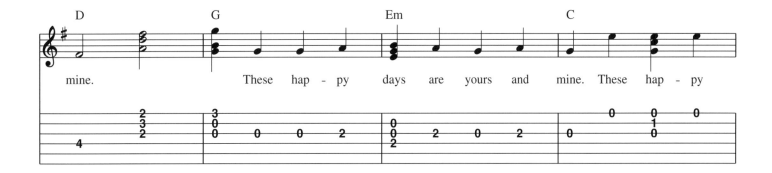

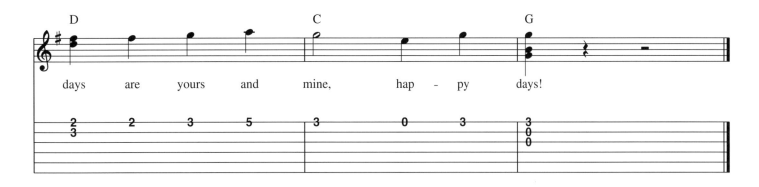

How to Save a Life

Words and Music by Joseph King and Isaac Slade

*Tune down 1 step:
(low to high) D – G – C – F – A – D

Strum Pattern: 3, 6
Pick Pattern: 4, 5

*Optional: To match recording, tune down 1 step.

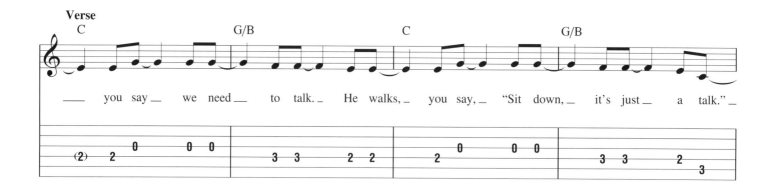

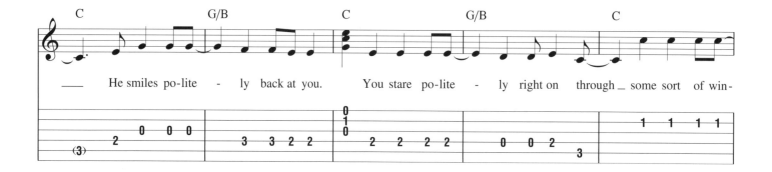

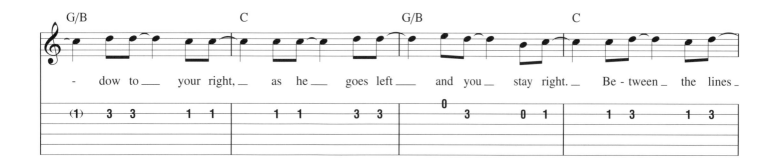

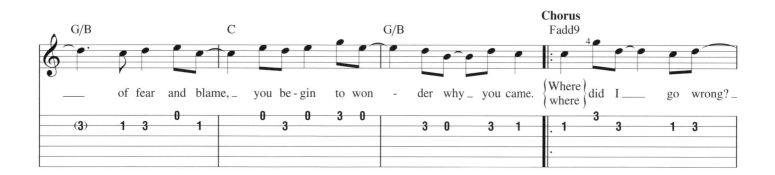

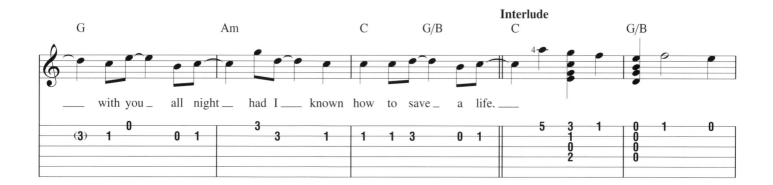

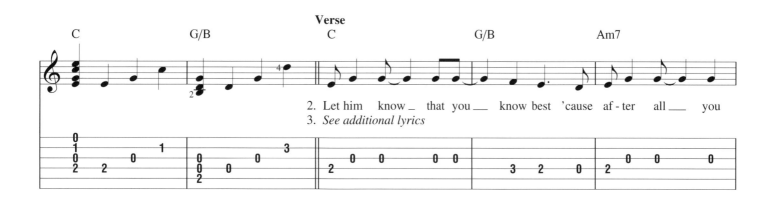

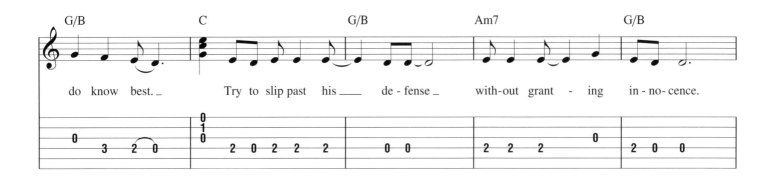

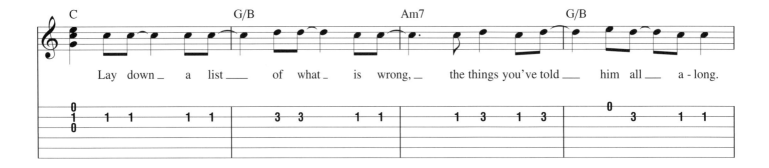

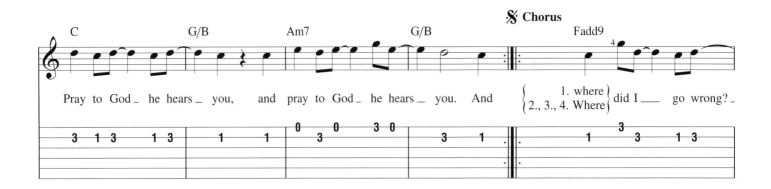

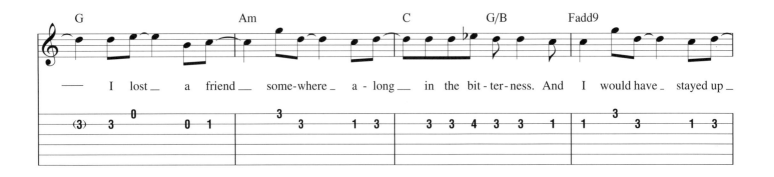

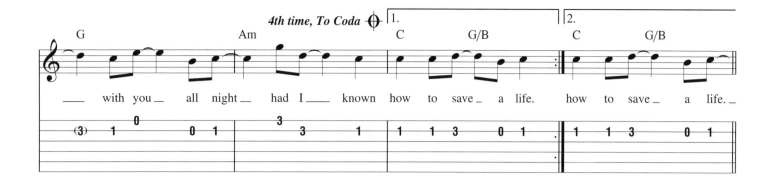

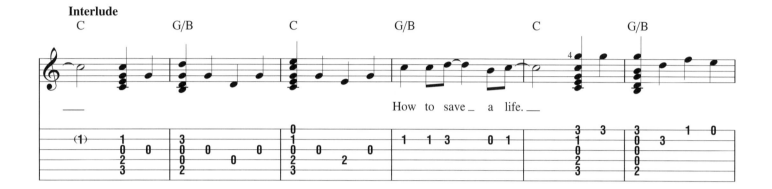

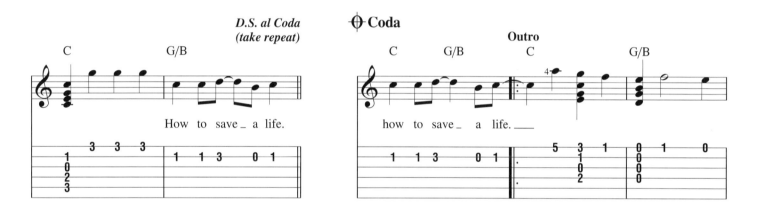

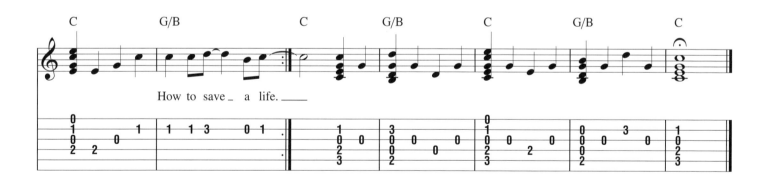

Additional Lyrics

3. As he begins to raise his voice,
   You lower yours and grant him one last choice.
   Drive until you lose the road
   Or break with the ones you've followed.
   He will do one of two things:
   He will admit to ev'rything,
   Or he'll say he's just not the same
   And you'll begin to wonder why you came.

Jesus Take the Wheel

Words and Music by Brett James, Gordie Sampson and Hillary Lindsey

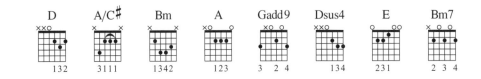

Strum Pattern: 1
Pick Pattern: 2

Intro
Moderately

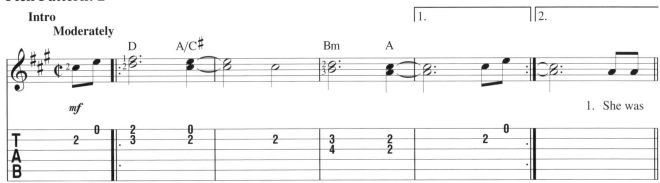

mf

1. She was

% Verse

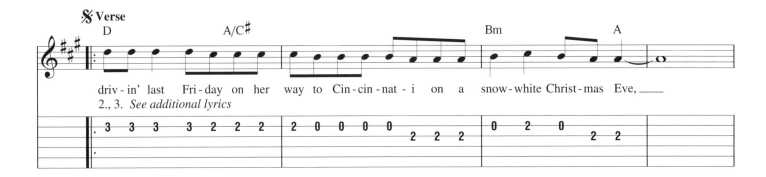

driv-in' last Fri-day on her way to Cin-cin-nat-i on a snow-white Christ-mas Eve, ___
2., 3. See additional lyrics

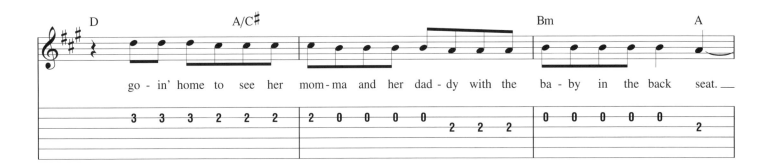

go-in' home to see her mom-ma and her dad-dy with the ba-by in the back seat. ___

To Coda 1

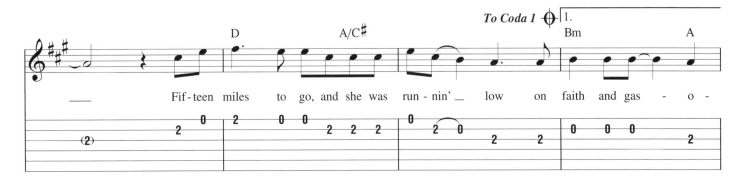

___ Fif-teen miles to go, and she was run-nin' ___ low on faith and gas - o -

*Sung one octave higher, next 11 meas.

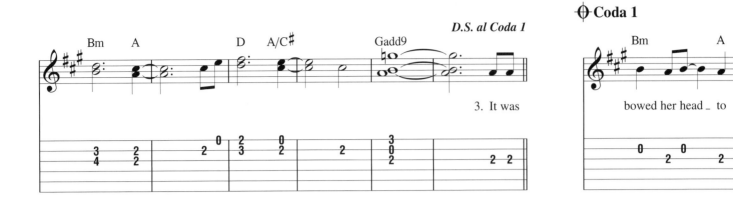

D.S. al Coda 1

3. It was   bowed her head _ to

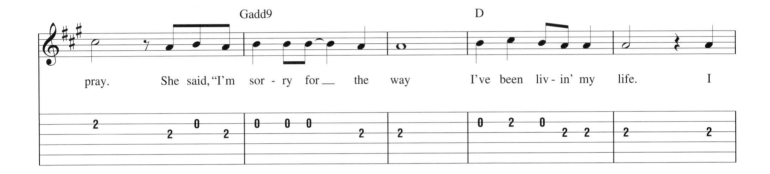

pray.   She said, "I'm sor - ry for __ the   way   I've been liv - in' my   life.   I

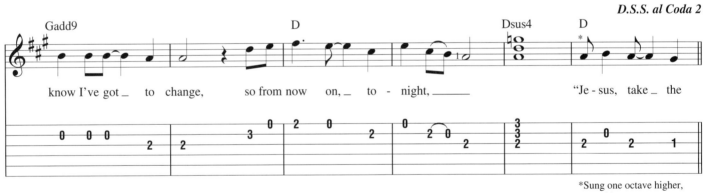

D.S.S. al Coda 2

know I've got _ to change,   so from now   on, _ to - night, _____   "Je - sus, take _ the

*Sung one octave higher, next 11 meas.

Coda 2

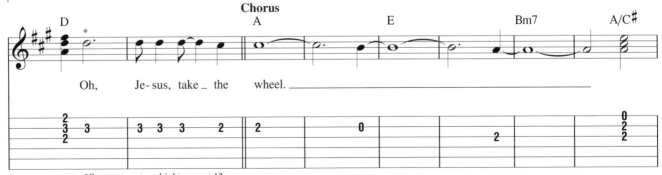

Chorus

Oh,   Je - sus, take _ the   wheel. _____

*Sung one octave highter, next 13 meas.

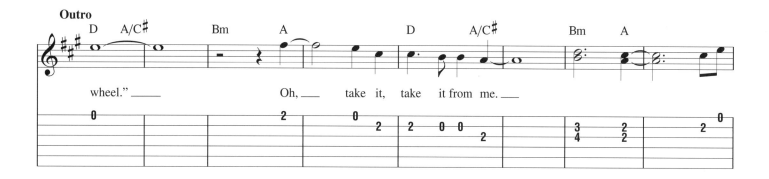

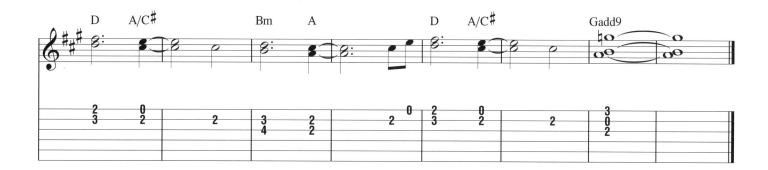

Additional Lyrics

2. She had a lot on her mind and she didn't pay attention.
   She was goin' way too fast,
   And before she knew it, she was spinning
   On a thin black sheet of glass.
   She saw both their lives flash before her eyes.
   She didn't even have time to cry.
   She was so scared. She threw her hands up in the air.

3. It was still getting colder when she made it to the shoulder
   And the car came to a stop.
   And she cried when she saw the baby in the back seat
   Sleeping like a rock.
   And for the first time in a long time
   She bowed her head to pray.
   She said, "I'm sorry for the way I've been livin' my life.
   I know I've got to change, so from now on, tonight..."

The Joker

Words and Music by Steve Miller, Eddie Curtis and Ahmet Ertegun

Strum Pattern: 3
Pick Pattern: 2

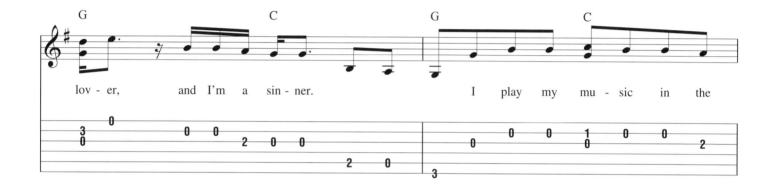

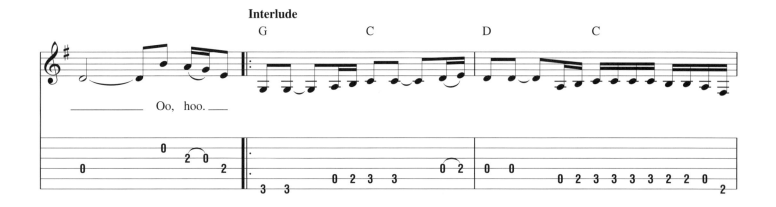

Oo, hoo.

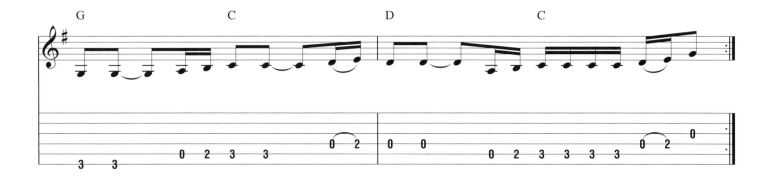

Verse

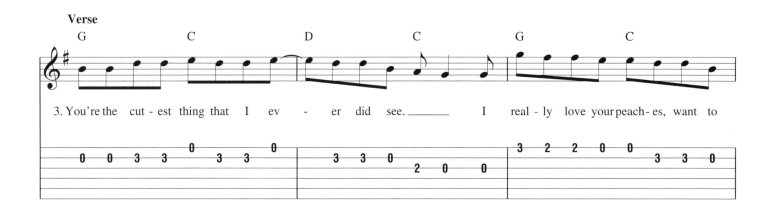

3. You're the cut - est thing that I ev - er did see._____ I real - ly love your peach - es, want to

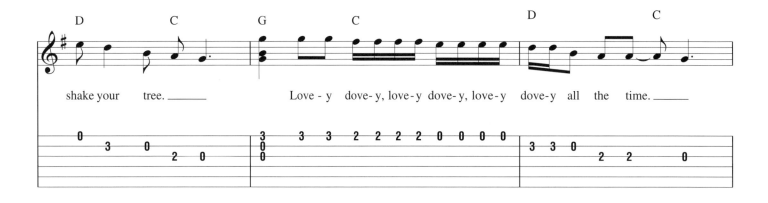

shake your tree._____ Love - y dove - y, love - y dove - y, love - y dove - y all the time._____

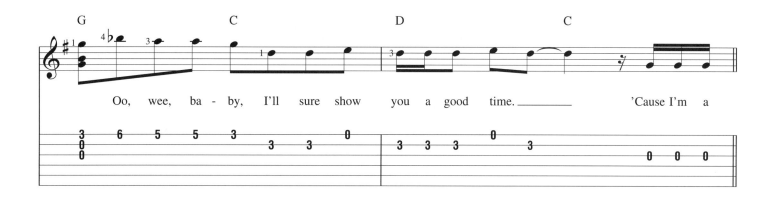

Oo, wee, ba - by, I'll sure show you a good time._____ 'Cause I'm a

Outro-Chorus

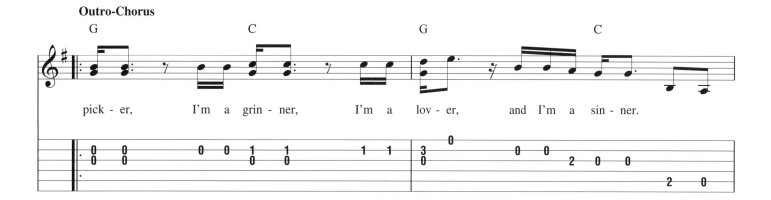

pick - er, I'm a grin - ner, I'm a lov - er, and I'm a sin - ner.

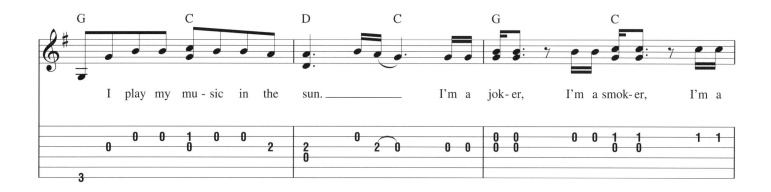

I play my mu - sic in the sun._____ I'm a jok - er, I'm a smok - er, I'm a

Repeat and fade

mid - night _ tok - er.

{ I get my lov - in' on the run._____ }
{ I sure don't wan - na hurt no one._____ }

I'm a

Love Shack

Words and Music by Catherine E. Pierson, Frederick W. Schneider, Keith J. Strickland and Cynthia L. Wilson

Strum Pattern: 5
Pick Pattern: 4

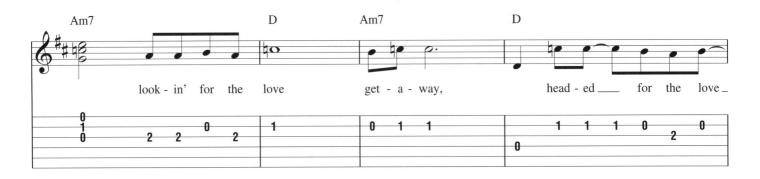

%. **Verse**

_____ get - a - way. 1. I got me a car,___ it's as big as a whale ___ and we're

3., 6. _See additional lyrics_

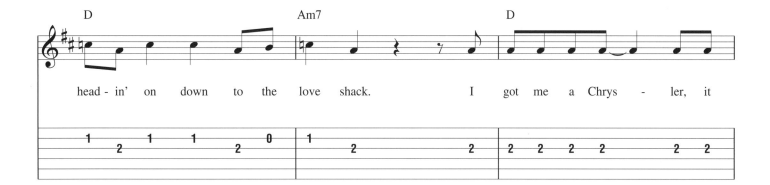

head - in' on down to the love shack. I got me a Chrys - ler, it

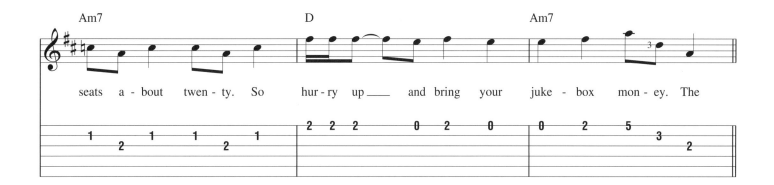

seats a - bout twen - ty. So hur - ry up ___ and bring your juke - box mon - ey. The

Chorus

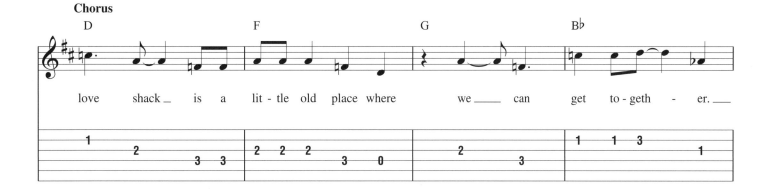

love shack ___ is a lit - tle old place where we ___ can get to - geth - er. ___

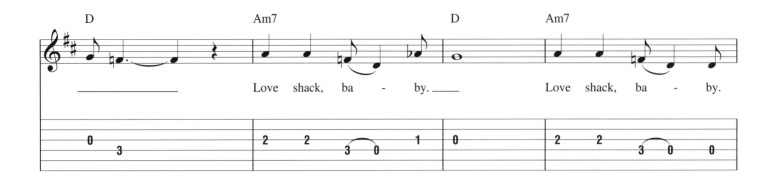

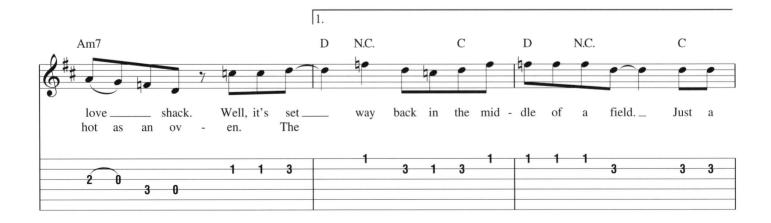

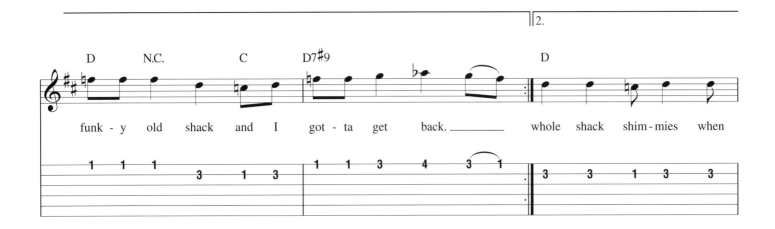

funk - y old shack and I got - ta get back. _____ whole shack shim - mies when

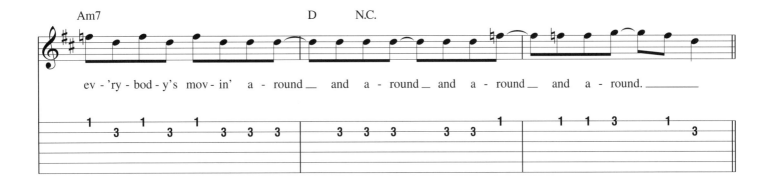

ev - 'ry - bod - y's mov - in' a - round _ and a - round _ and a - round _ and a - round. _____

Verse

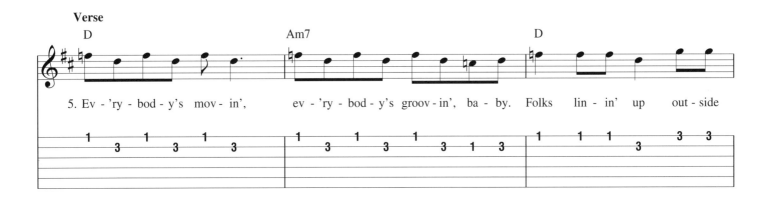

5. Ev - 'ry - bod - y's mov - in', ev - 'ry - bod - y's groov - in', ba - by. Folks lin - in' up out - side

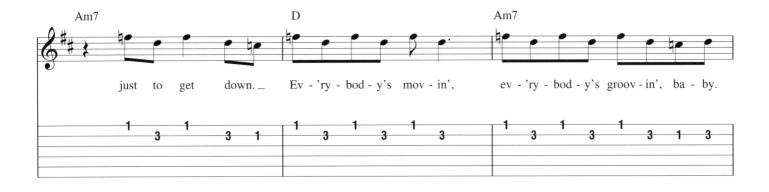

just to get down. _ Ev - 'ry - bod - y's mov - in', ev - 'ry - bod - y's groov - in', ba - by.

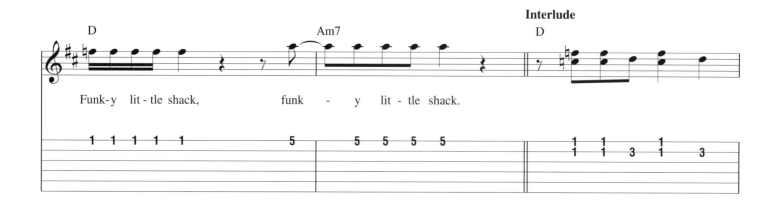

Funk-y lit-tle shack, funk - y lit-tle shack.

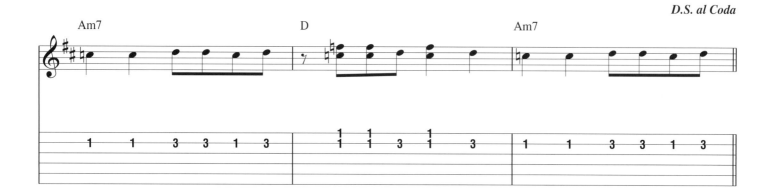

D.S. al Coda

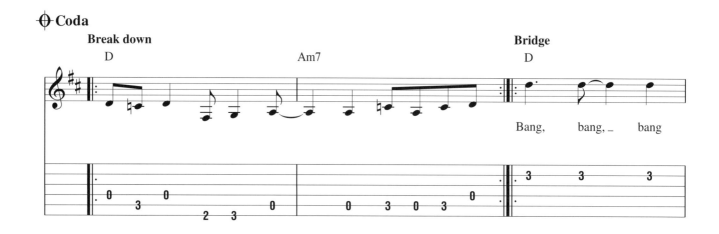

Coda

Bang, bang,__ bang

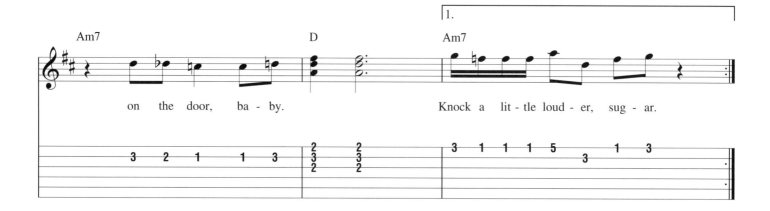

on the door, ba - by. Knock a lit-tle loud-er, sug - ar.

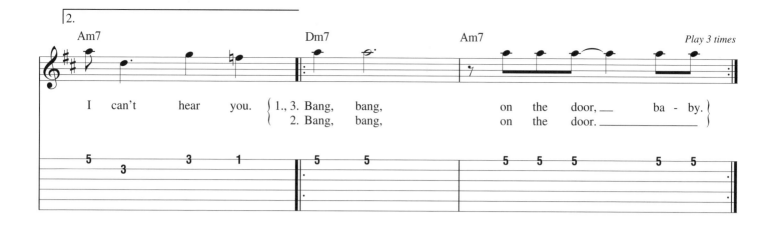

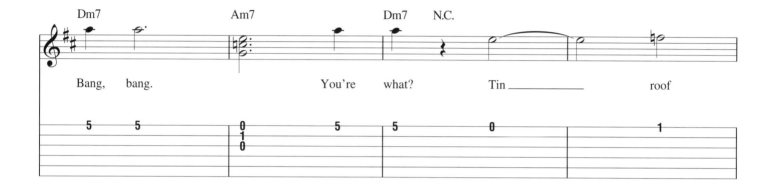

Outro

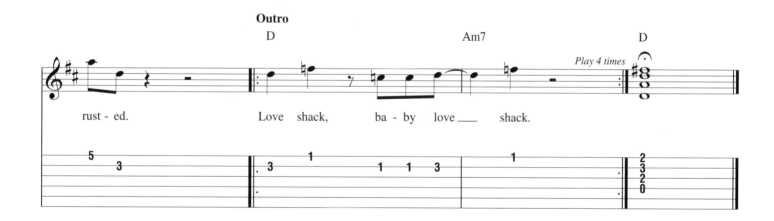

Additional Lyrics

3. Glitter on the mattress, glitter on the highway.
   Glitter on the front porch, glitter on the hallway.

6. Hop in my Chrysler, it's as big as a whale
   And it's about to set sail.
   I got me a car, it seats about twenty.
   So hurry up and bring your jukebox money.

Nights in White Satin

Words and Music by Justin Hayward

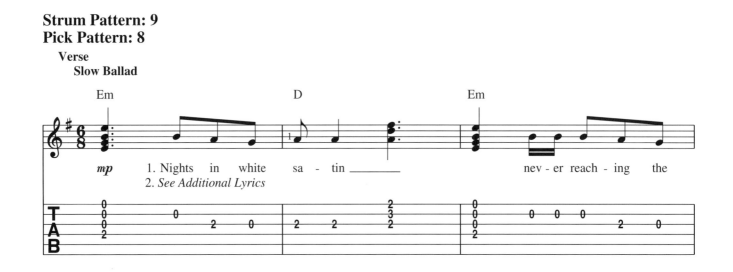

Strum Pattern: 9
Pick Pattern: 8

Verse
Slow Ballad

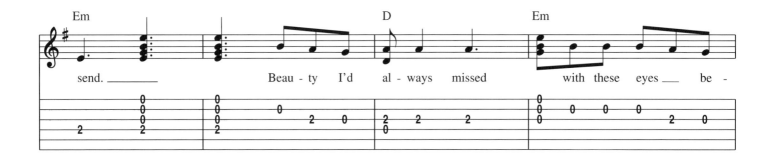

1. Nights in white sa - tin _____ nev - er reach - ing the
2. *See Additional Lyrics*

end. _____ Let - ters I've writ - ten, _____ nev - er mean - ing to

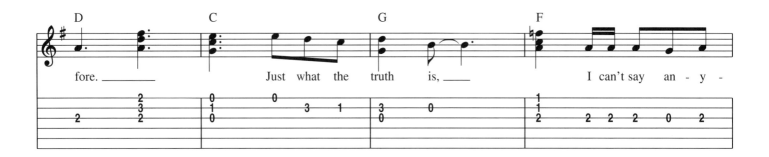

send. _____ Beau - ty I'd al - ways missed with these eyes ___ be -

fore. _____ Just what the truth is, ___ I can't say an - y -

Chorus

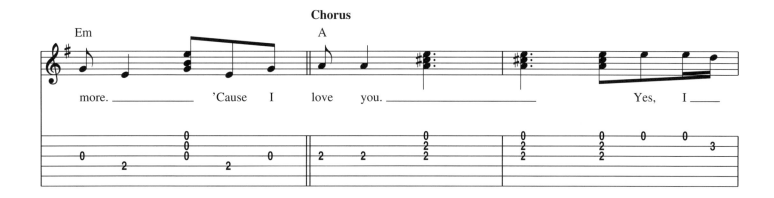

more. _____ 'Cause I love you. _____ Yes, I _____

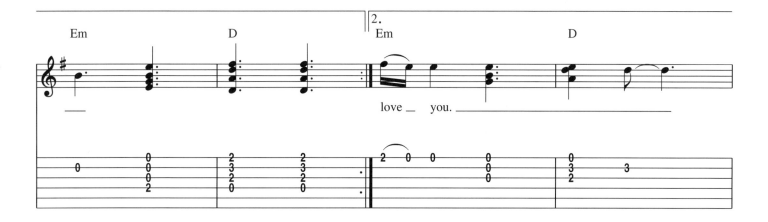

love you. _____ Oh, _____ how I love _ you. _____

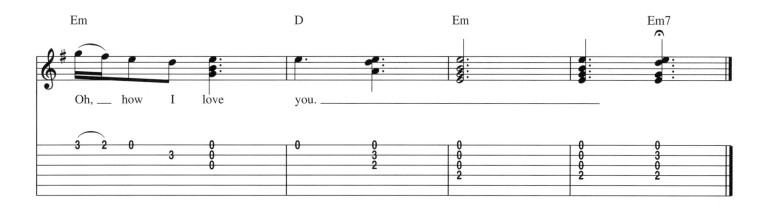

_____ love _ you. _____

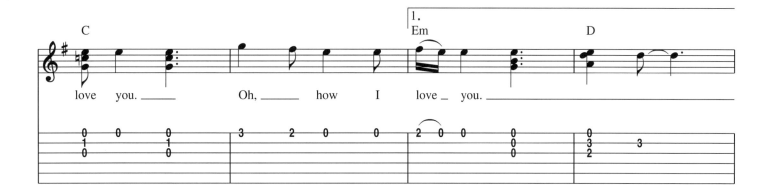

Oh, _ how I love you. _____

Additional Lyrics

2. Gazing at people, some hand in hand.
Just what I'm going through, they can't understand.
Some try to tell me thoughts they can not defend.
Just what you want to be, you'll be in the end.
And I…

Papa Was a Rollin' Stone

Words and Music by Norman Whitfield and Barrett Strong

Am7

Strum Pattern: 1, 2
Pick Pattern: 4, 5

Verse
Moderately fast

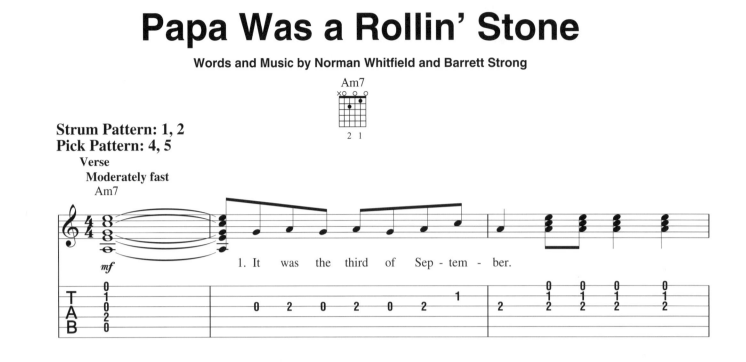

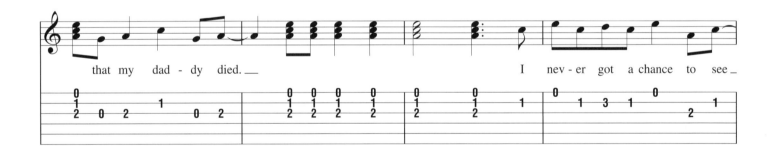

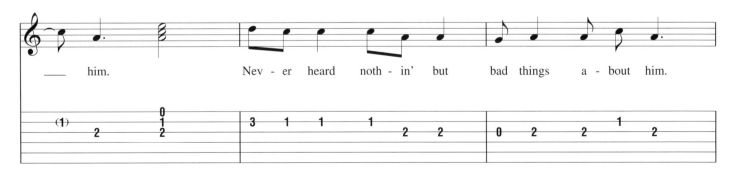

Ma-ma, I'm de-pend-ing on you to tell me the truth. _ *Spoken: Mama just hung her head and said, "Son,*

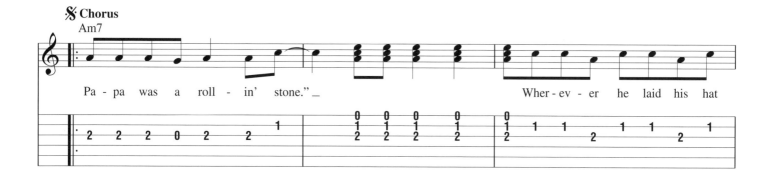

𝄋 Chorus

Am7

Pa - pa was a roll - in' stone." _ Wher - ev - er he laid his hat

was his home. _ And when he died, _ all he left _ us was a -

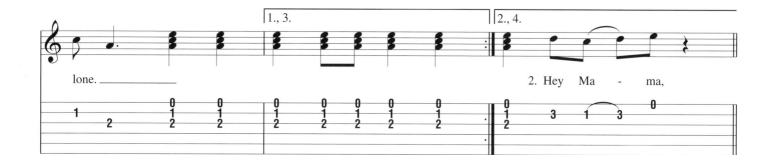

lone. _____ 2. Hey Ma - ma,

Verse

Am7

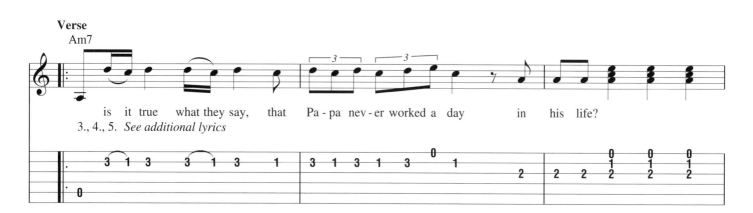

is it true what they say, that Pa - pa nev - er worked a day in his life?

3., 4., 5. *See additional lyrics*

Additional Lyrics

3. Heard some talk about Papa doin' some storefront preachin.'
   Talkin' 'bout savin' souls and the time preaching,
   Healing and then stealing in the name of the Lord.

4. I heard Papa call himself a jack-of-all-trades.
   Tell me, is that what sent Papa to an early grave?
   Folks say Papa would beg, borrow, steal to pay his bills.

5. Hey Mama, folks say Papa was never much on thinkin',
   Spent most of his time chasin' women and drinkin'.
   Mama, I'm depending on you to tell me the truth.

Ring of Fire

Words and Music by Merle Kilgore and June Carter

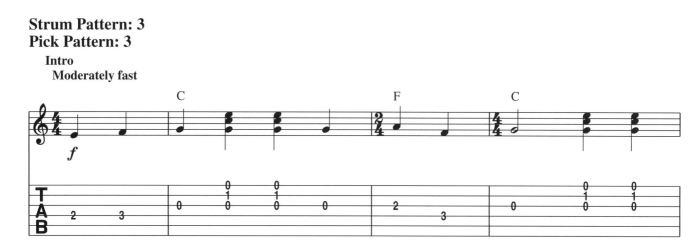

Strum Pattern: 3
Pick Pattern: 3

Intro
Moderately fast

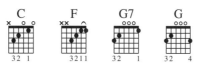

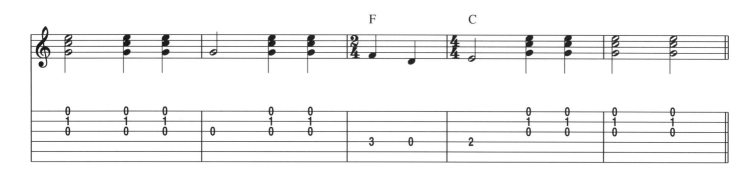

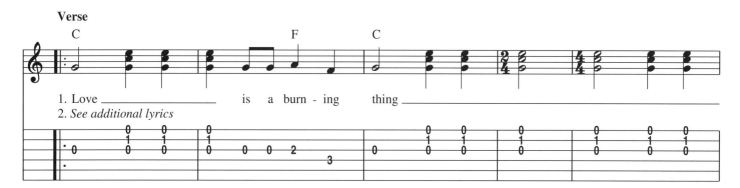

Verse

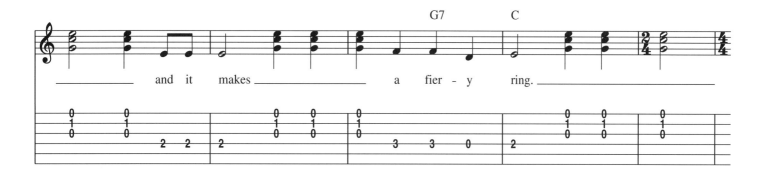

1. Love _____ is a burn - ing thing _____
2. *See additional lyrics*

_____ and it makes _____ a fier - y ring. _____

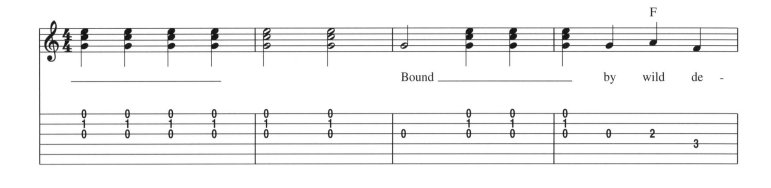

Bound _____ by wild de-

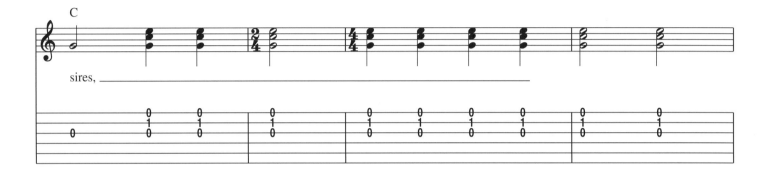

sires, _____

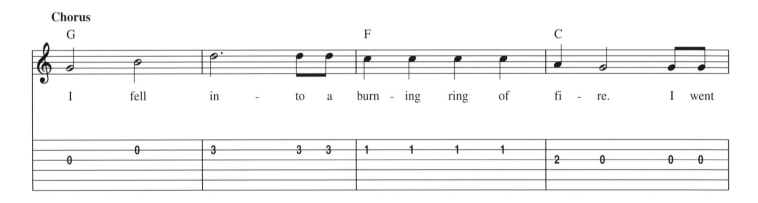

I fell in - to a ring of fire, _____

Chorus

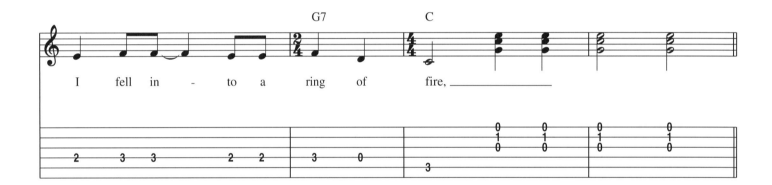

I fell in - to a burn - ing ring of fi - re. I went

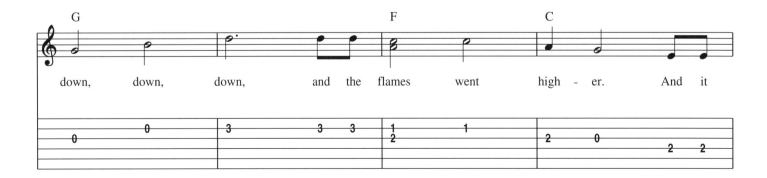

down, down, down, and the flames went high - er. And it

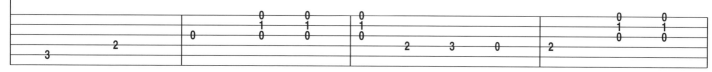

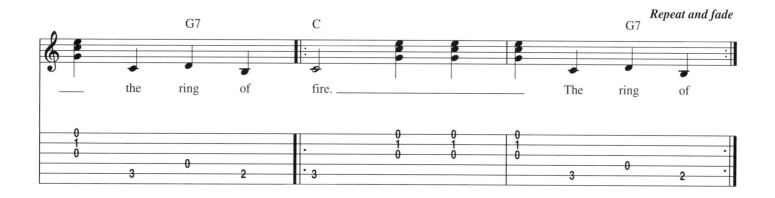

Additional Lyrics

2. The taste of love is sweet
When hearts like ours beat.
I fell for you like a child.
Oh, but the fire went wild.

Rock Me Baby

Words and Music by B.B. King and Joe Bihari

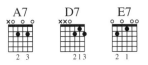

Strum Pattern: 1, 2
Pick Pattern: 2, 4

Intro

Slowly

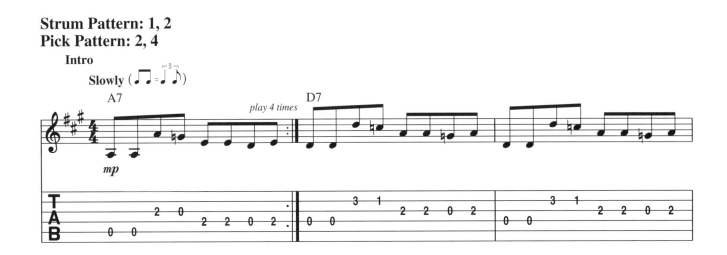

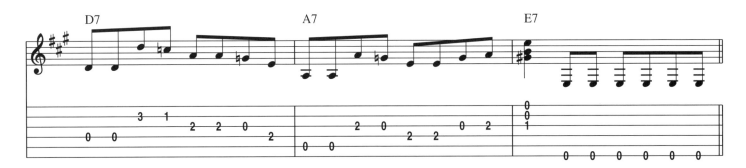

Verse

1. Rock me,   ba - by,   rock me   all ___ night   long. ___
2., 3. *See Additional Lyrics*

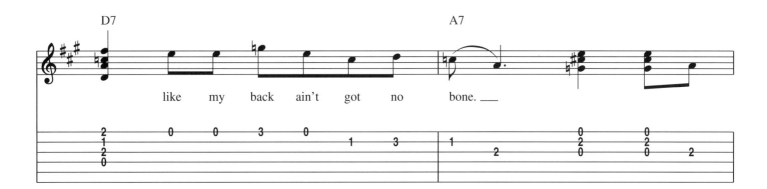

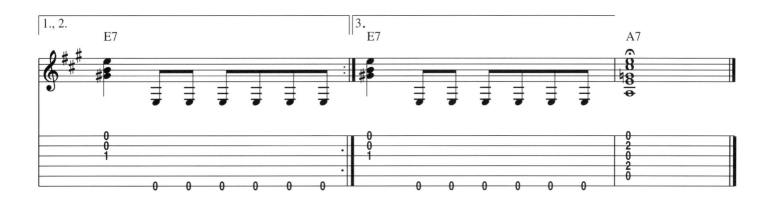

Additional Lyrics

2. Roll me, baby, like you roll a wagon wheel.
   Want you to roll me, baby, like you roll a wagon wheel.
   Want you to roll me, baby, you don't know how it makes me feel.

3. Rock me, baby, honey, rock me slow.
   Hey, rock me, pretty baby, baby, rock me slow.
   Will you rock me, baby, 'til I want no more?

St. Elsewhere

from the Television Series ST. ELSEWHERE
By Dave Grusin

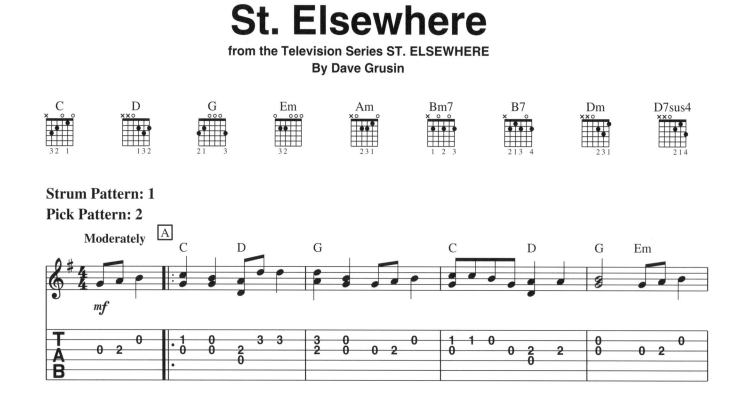

Strum Pattern: 1
Pick Pattern: 2

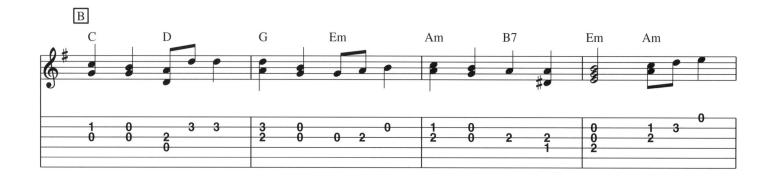

Space Oddity

Words and Music by David Bowie

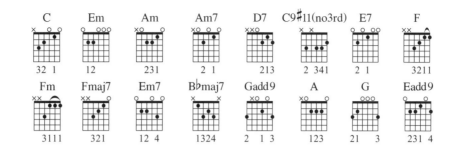

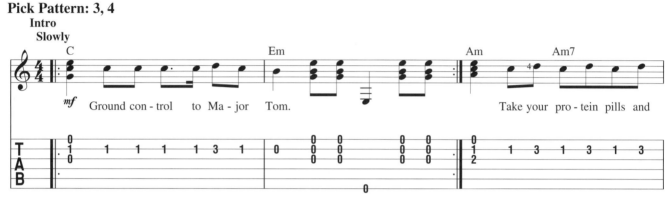

Strum Pattern: 2, 3
Pick Pattern: 3, 4

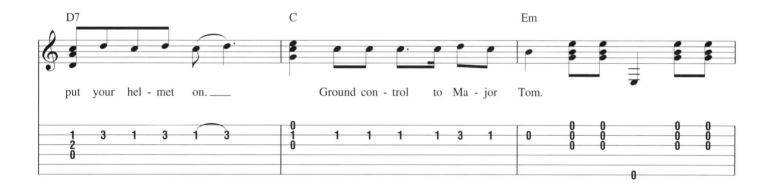

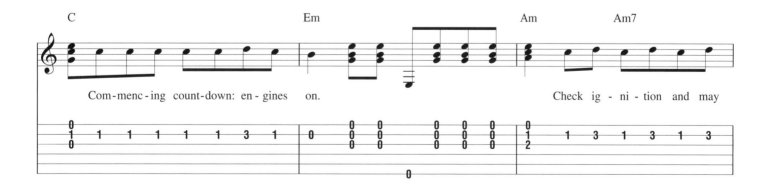

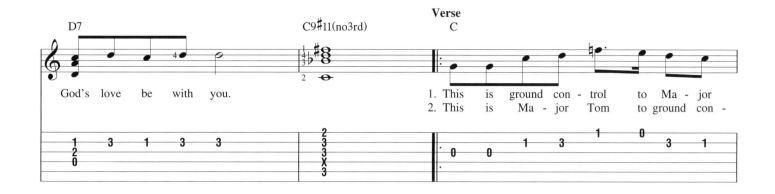

God's love be with you.

Verse

1. This is ground con - trol to Ma - jor
2. This is Ma - jor Tom to ground con -

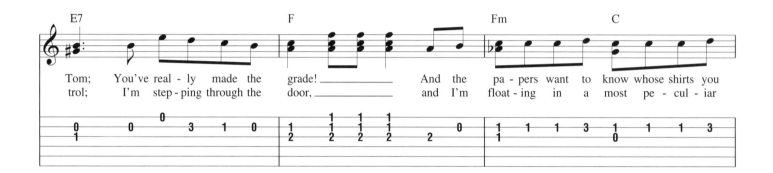

Tom; You've real - ly made the grade!_____ And the pa - pers want to know whose shirts you
trol; I'm step - ping through the door,_____ and I'm float - ing in a most pe - cul - iar

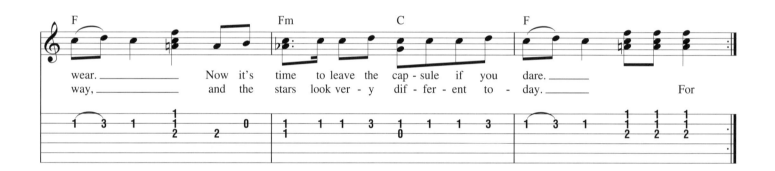

wear._____ Now it's time to leave the cap - sule if you dare._____
way,_____ and the stars look ver - y dif - fer - ent to - day._____ For

% Bridge

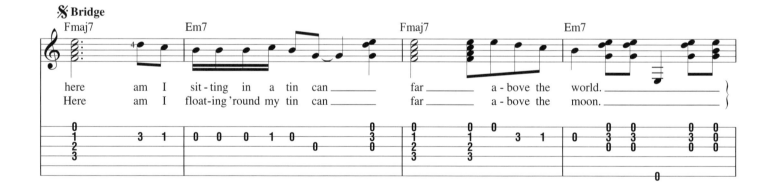

here am I sit - ting in a tin can _____ far _____ a - bove the world. _____
Here am I float - ing 'round my tin can _____ far _____ a - bove the moon. _____

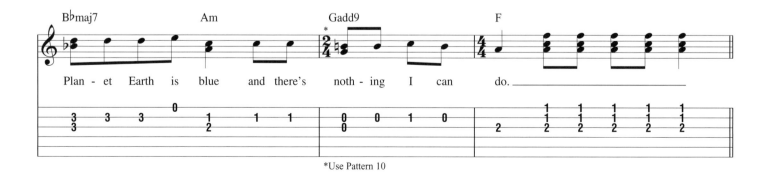

Plan - et Earth is blue and there's noth - ing I can do. _____

*Use Pattern 10

138

Interlude

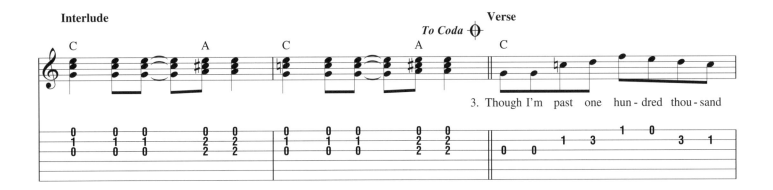

miles I'm feel - ing ver - y still. _____ And I think my space - ship knows which way to

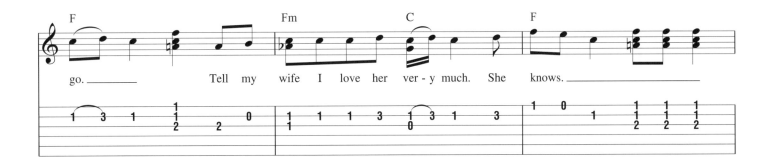

go. _____ Tell my wife I love her ver - y much. She knows. _____

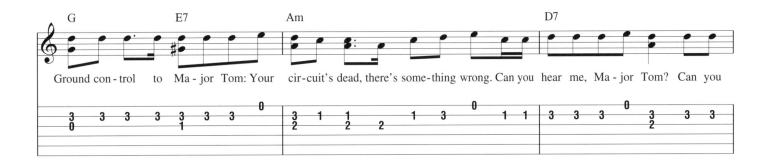

Ground con - trol to Ma - jor Tom: Your cir - cuit's dead, there's some - thing wrong. Can you hear me, Ma - jor Tom? Can you

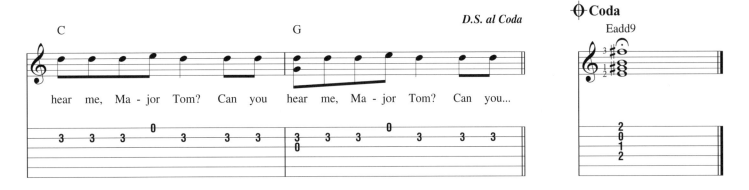

hear me, Ma - jor Tom? Can you hear me, Ma - jor Tom? Can you...

Tainted Love

Words and Music by Ed Cobb

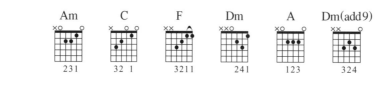

*Tune down 1 step:
(low to high) D–G–C–F–A–D

Strum Pattern: 3, 4
Pick Pattern: 4, 5

Intro
Moderately

*Optional: To match recording, tune down 1 step.

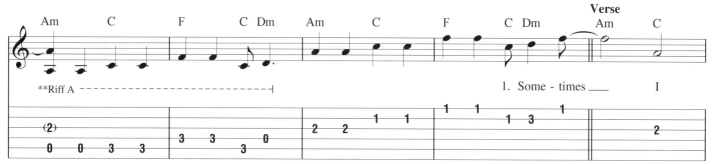

**Riff A is basic accompaniment throughout Verse,
Chorus, and Bridge. Chord symbols are implied.

1. Some - times ___ I

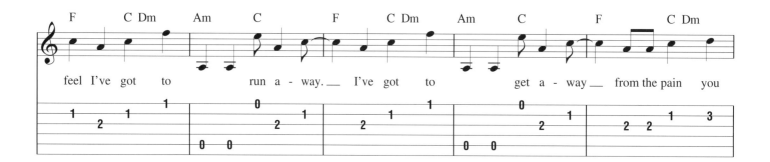

feel I've got to   run a - way. ___ I've got to   get a - way ___ from the pain you

drive ___ in - to the heart ___ of me. ___ The love ___ we   share ___ seems to go no -

§ **Pre-Chorus**

*Strum chords

To Coda ⊕

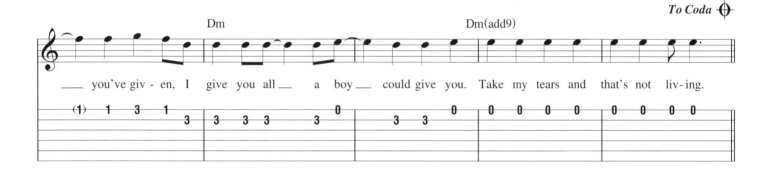

Chorus ... **Verse**

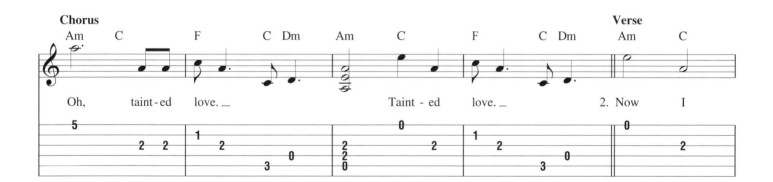

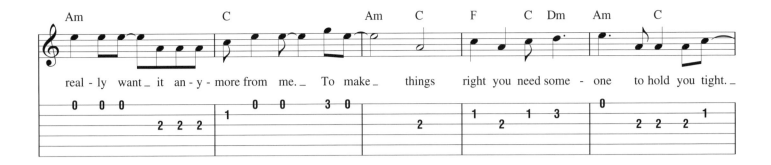

real - ly want — it an - y - more from me. — To make — things right you need some - one to hold you tight. —

D.S. al Coda

— And you'll think love is to pray. ——— But I'm sor - ry, I don't pray that way.

⊕ Coda
Chorus

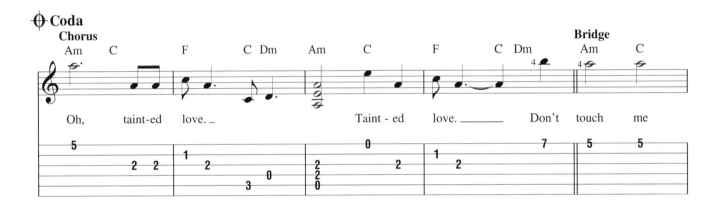

Oh, taint - ed love. — Taint - ed love. ——— Don't touch me

Bridge

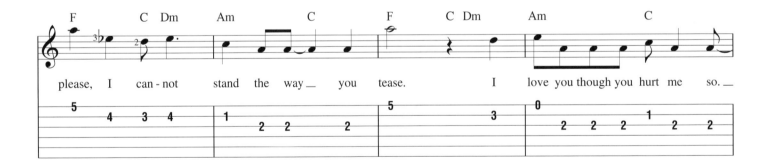

please, I can - not stand the way — you tease. I love you though you hurt me so. —

Outro-Chorus

Repeat and fade

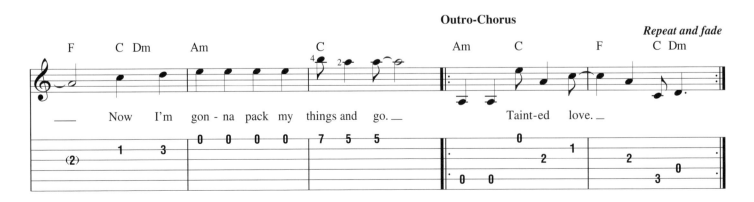

— Now I'm gon - na pack my things and go. — Taint-ed love.

Zombie

Lyrics and Music by Dolores O'Riordan

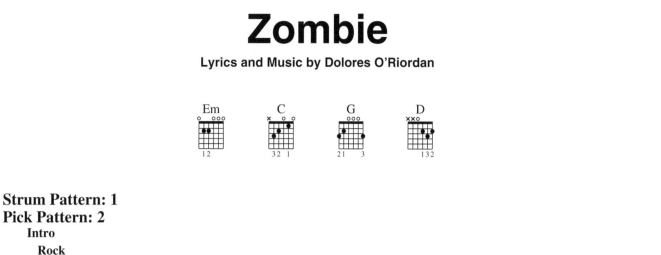

Strum Pattern: 1
Pick Pattern: 2

Intro

Rock

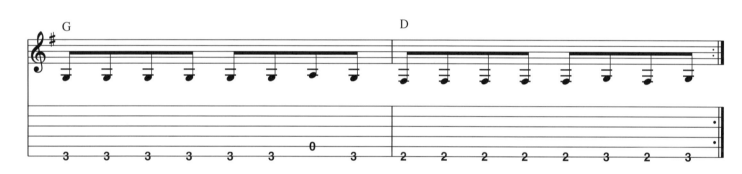

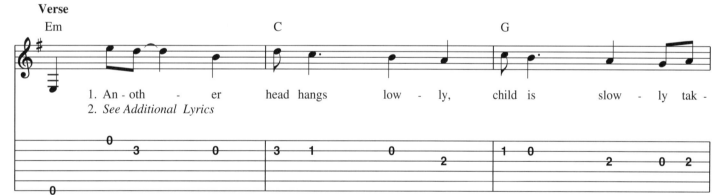

Verse

1. An - oth - er head hangs low - ly, child is slow - ly tak -
2. *See Additional Lyrics*

en. And the vi - 'lence caused such si - lence,

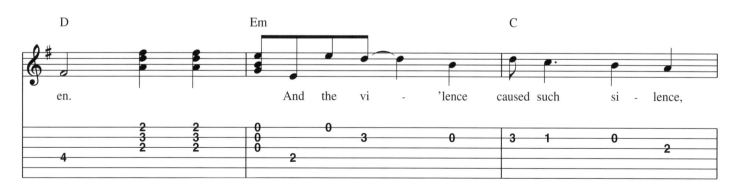

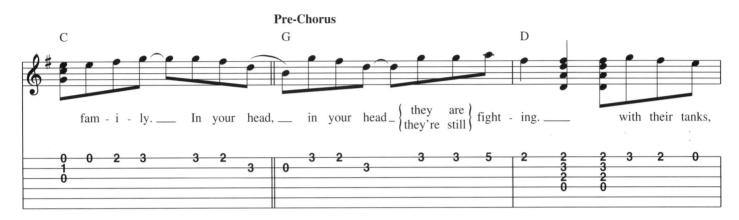

Pre-Chorus

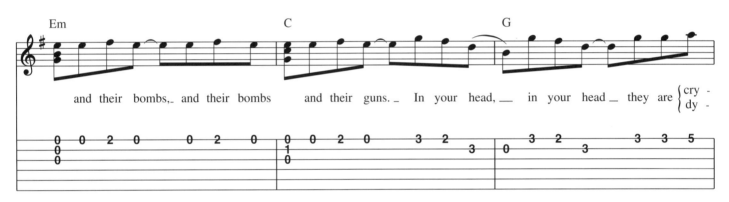

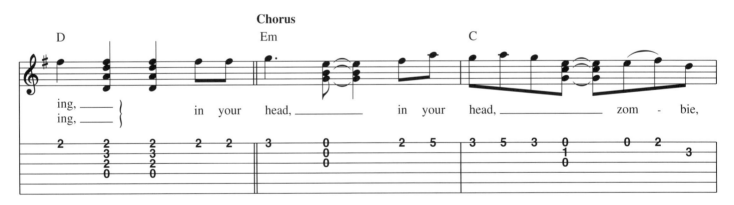

Chorus

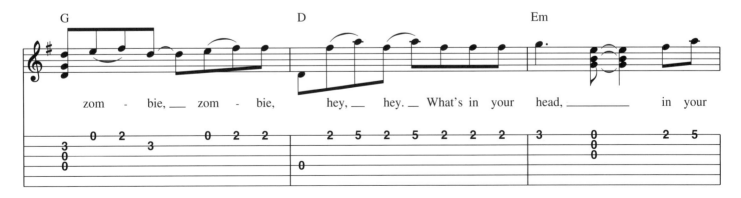

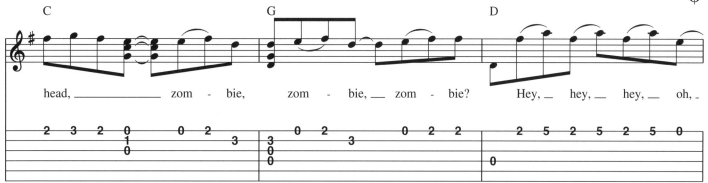

head, _____ zom - bie, zom - bie, __ zom - bie? Hey, __ hey, __ hey, __ oh, _

D.C. al Coda

__ doo, doo, doo, doo, doo, doo, doo, doo, doo, doo, doo, doo, doo, doo, doo, doo.

⊕ *Coda*

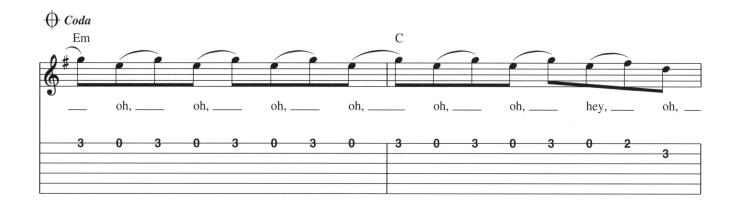

__ oh, ___ oh, ___ oh, ___ oh, ___ oh, ___ oh, ___ hey, ___ Oh, __

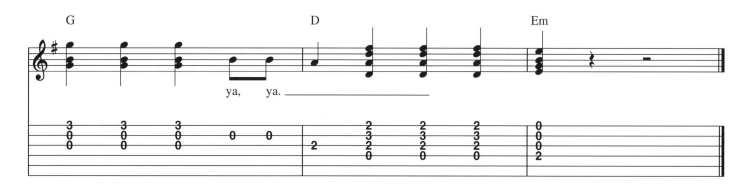

ya, ya. _____

Additional Lyrics

2. Another mother's breakin' heart is taking over.
When the vi'lence causes silence,
We must be mistaken.
It's the same old theme since nineteen-sixteen.

145

The Twist

Words and Music by Hank Ballard

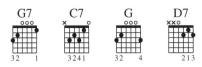

Strum Pattern: 3
Pick Pattern: 3

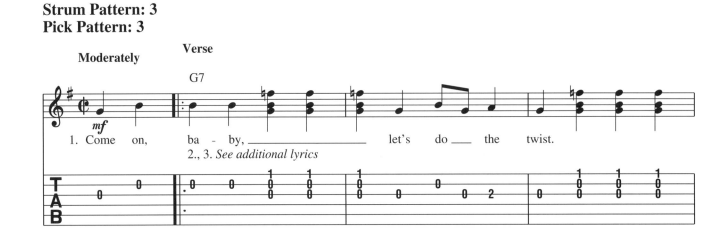

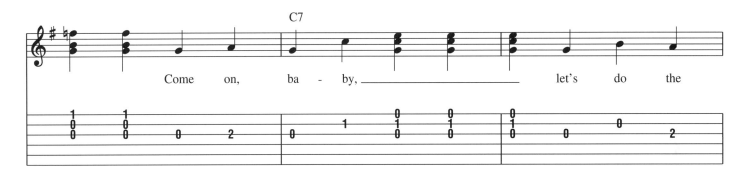

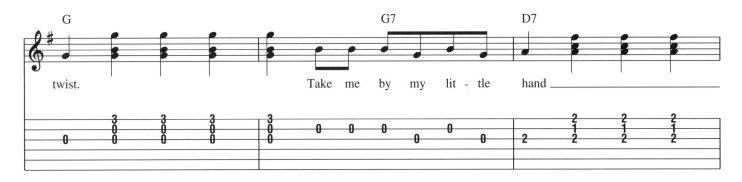

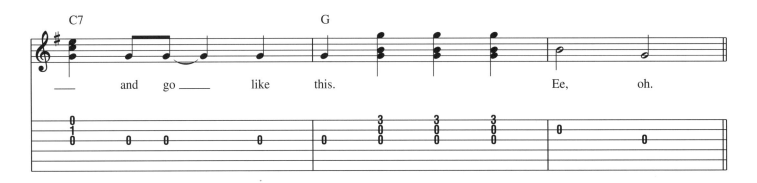

Chorus

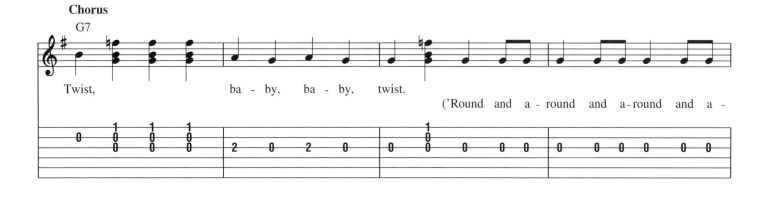

Twist, ba - by, ba - by, twist. ('Round and a - round and a - round and a -

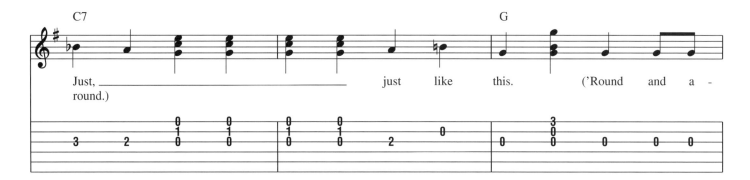

Just, _____ just like this. ('Round and a -
round.)

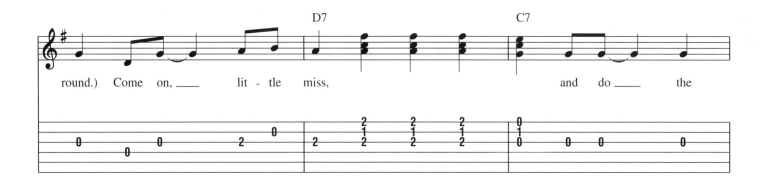

round.) Come on, ___ lit - tle miss, and do ___ the

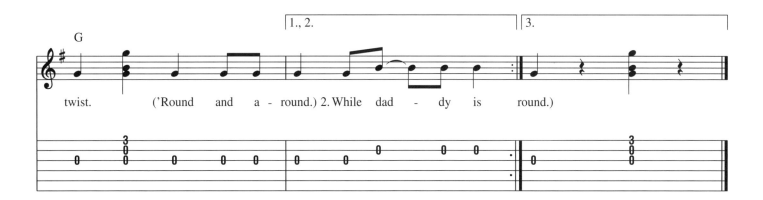

twist. ('Round and a - round.) 2. While dad - dy is round.)

Additional Lyrics

2. While daddy is sleeping and mama ain't around.
   While daddy is sleeping and mama ain't around.
   We're gonna twisty, twisty, twisty
   Until we tear the house down.

3. You should see my little sis.
   You should see my little sis.
   She knows how to rock
   And she knows how to twist.

You'll Never Walk Alone

from CAROUSEL
Lyrics by Oscar Hammerstein II
Music by Richard Rodgers

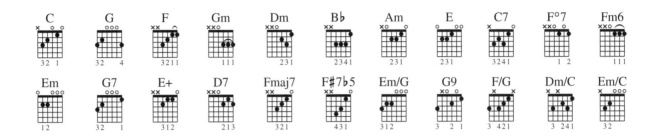

Strum Pattern: 4
Pick Pattern: 2

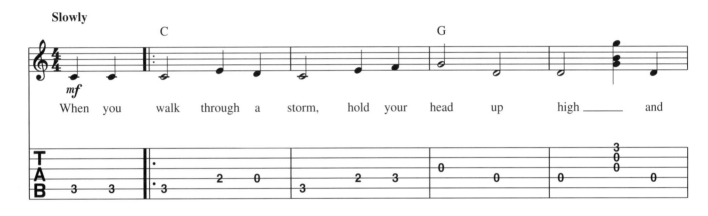

Slowly

When you walk through a storm, hold your head up high _____ and

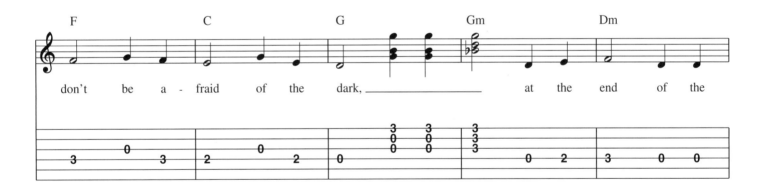

don't be a - fraid of the dark, _____ at the end of the

storm is a gold - en sky and the sweet sil - ver song of a

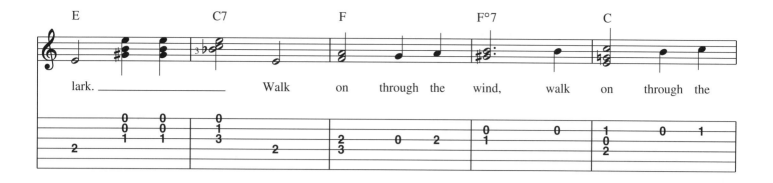

lark. _____ Walk on through the wind, walk on through the

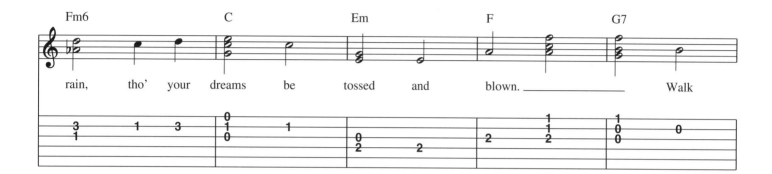

rain, tho' your dreams be tossed and blown. _____ Walk

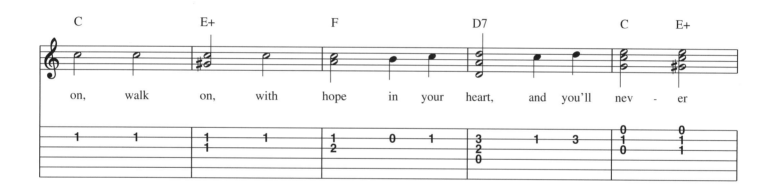

on, walk on, with hope in your heart, and you'll nev - er

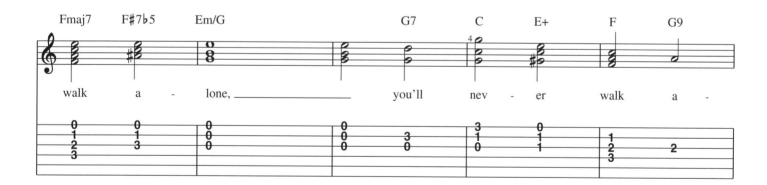

walk a - lone, _____ you'll nev - er walk a -

lone! _____ When you lone! _____

Alright, Okay, You Win

Words and Music by Sid Wyche and Mayme Watts

Strum Pattern: 4
Pick Pattern: 1

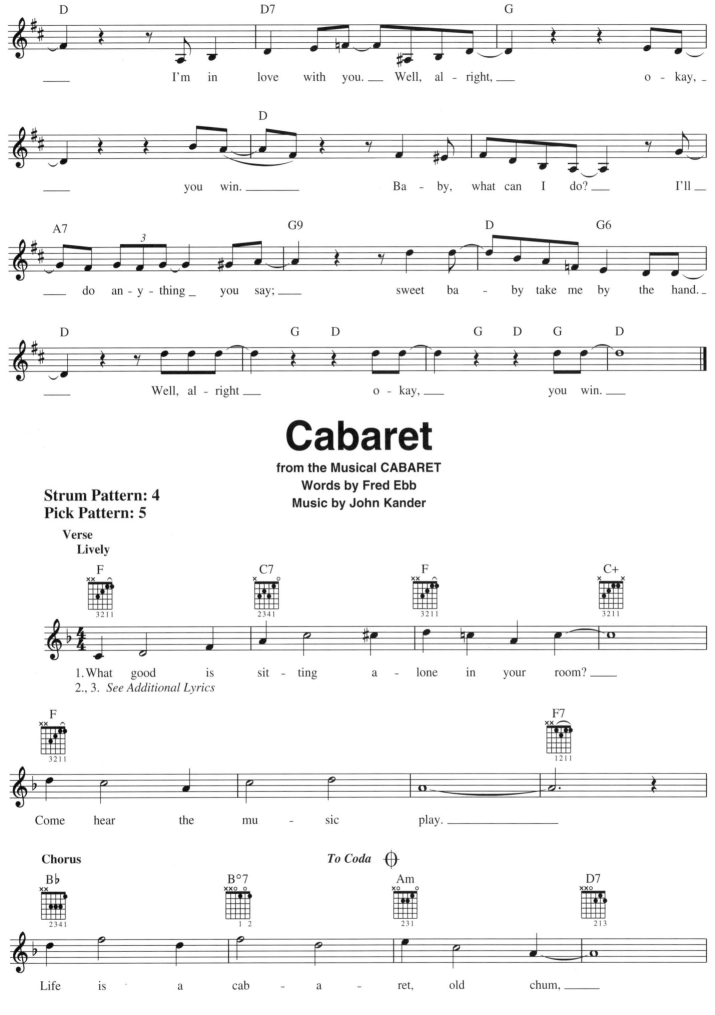

Cabaret

from the Musical CABARET
Words by Fred Ebb
Music by John Kander

Strum Pattern: 4
Pick Pattern: 5

Verse
Lively

F C7 F C+

1. What good is sit - ting a - lone in your room? ____
2., 3. *See Additional Lyrics*

F F7

Come hear the mu - sic play. ____

Chorus
To Coda

B♭ B°7 Am D7

Life is a cab - a - ret, old chum, ____

Additional Lyrics

2. Put down the knitting, the book and the broom,
   Time for a holiday.

3. No use permitting some prophet of doom
   To wipe ev'ry smile away.

Barbara Ann

Words and Music by Fred Fassert

Always Be My Baby

Words and Music by Mariah Carey, Jermaine Dupri and Manuel Seal

Additional Lyrics

2. I ain't gonna cry, no, and I won't beg you to stay.
   If you're determined to leave boy, I will not stand in your way.
   But inevitably you'll be back agian,
   'Cause you know in your heart, babe, our love will never end.

At the Hop

Words and Music by Arthur Singer, John Madara and David White

Additional Lyrics

2. Well, you can swing it, you can groove it,
   You can really start to move it at the hop.
   Where the jockey is the smoothest
   And the music is the coolest at the hop.
   All the cats and the chicks can get their kicks at the hop.

4. You can swing it, you can groove it,
   You can really start to move it at the hop.
   Where the jockey is the smoothest
   And the music is the coolest at the hop.
   All the cats and the chicks can get their kicks at the hop.
   Spoken: Let's go!

Book of Love

Words and Music by Warren Davis, George Malone and Charles Patrick

Strum Pattern: 6
Pick Pattern: 6

Verse

Brightly

1. Tell me, tell me, tell me, oh, who wrote the book of love? I've got to know the
2., 3. *See additional lyrics*

an-swer, was it some-one from a-bove? I won-der, won-der who,____

who, who wrote the book of love? Chap-ter One says to

love her, to love her with all your heart. Chap-ter Two you tell her, you're

nev-er, nev-er, nev-er, nev-er, ev-er gon-na part. In Chap-ter Three re-mem-ber the

mean-ing of ro-mance. In Chap-ter Four you break up, but you give her just one more

chance. Oh, I won-der won-der who,____ who,

who wrote the book of love? love?____

Additional Lyrics

2. I love you, darling,
   Baby, you know I do.
   But I've got to see this book of love,
   Find out why it's true.

3. Baby, baby, baby,
   I love you, yes, I do.
   Well, it says so in this book of love,
   Ours is the one that's true.

Come Together

Words and Music by John Lennon and Paul McCartney

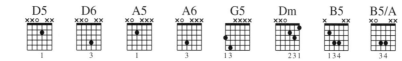

Strum Pattern: 1

Verse
Slow Rock

1. Here come old flat-top, he come groov-in' up slow-ly. He got
2., 3., 4. *See additional lyrics*

Joo Joo eye-ball, he one ho-ly roll-er. He got hair down

to his knee. _ Got to be a jok-er, he just do what he please. _

got to be free. Come to-geth-er right now, _____ o-ver

me.

4.

Chorus

B5   B5/A   G5   A5

so hard to see.___ Come to-geth-er right now,_____ o-ver

Dm

me.

Outro   *Repeat and fade*

D5 D6   D5 D6   D5 D6   D5 D6   D5 D6   D5 D6   D5 D6   D5 D6

Come to-geth-er,   yeah.   *Additional Lyrics*   Come to-geth-er,   yeah.

2. He wear no shoeshine, he got
Toe jam football. He got
Monkey finger, he shoot
Coca Cola. He say,
"I know you, you know me."
One thing I can tell you is you got to be free.

3. He bag production, he got
Walrus gumboot. He got
Ono sideboard, he one
Spinal cracker. He got
Feet down below his knee.
Hold you in his armchair you can feel his disease.

4. He roller coaster, he got
Early warning. He got
Muddy water, he one
Mojo filter. He say,
"One and one and one is three."
Got to be good looking 'cause he so hard to see.

Don't Stand So Close to Me

Music and Lyrics by Sting

F/A   G   Am   D   A   Bm   Em/A

Strum Pattern: 2
Pick Pattern: 3

Verse
Bright Rock

F/A   G   Am   G   Am

1. Young tea-cher,   the sub-ject   of school-girl fan-ta-sy.___
2., 3. *See Additional Lyrics.*

F/A   G   Am   G   Am

She wants him so bad-ly, knows what she wants to be.___

Additional Lyrics

2. Her friends are so jealous.
   You know how bad girls get.
   Sometimes it's not so easy,
   To be the teacher's pet.
   Temptation, frustration,
   So bad it makes him cry.
   Wet bus stop, she's waiting.
   His car is warm and dry.

3. Loose talk in the classroom,
   To hurt they try and try.
   Strong talk in the staff room,
   The accusations fly.
   It's no use, he sees her.
   He starts to shake and cough,
   Just like the old man in
   That book by Nabakov.

God Bless' the Child

Words and Music by Arthur Herzog Jr. and Billie Holiday

Strum Pattern: 4
Pick Pattern: 5

Additional Lyrics

2. Yes, the strong gets more, while the weak ones fade,
Empty pockets don't ever make the grade.
Mama may have, Papa may have,
But God bless' the child that's got his own!
That's got his own.

3. Rich relations give, crust of bread, and such,
You can help yourself, but don't take too much!
Mama may have, Papa may have,
But God bless' the child that's got his own!
That's got his own.

I Can See for Miles

Words and Music by Peter Townshend

Strum Pattern: 2
Pick Pattern: 1

Well here's a poke at you, __ you're gon-na choke on it too. __ You're gon-na

Chorus

lose that smile _ be - cause all the while _____ I could see for miles and

miles. I could see for miles and miles. I can see for miles and miles and

miles and miles and miles. _____ Oh, yeah. _____

1.

2. **Interlude**

play 3 times

D.S. al Coda

4. I

⊕ Coda

Verse

5. The Eif - fel Tower and the Taj Ma - hal are mine to see on clear days. _

You thought that I would need a crys - tal ball to see right through the haze. _

Well here's a poke at you, __ you're gon - na choke on it too. __ You're gon - na

lose that smile, __ be - cause all the while _____ I could see for miles and

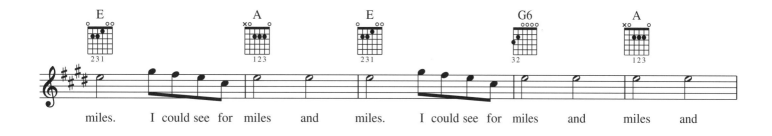

miles. I could see for miles and miles. I could see for miles and miles and

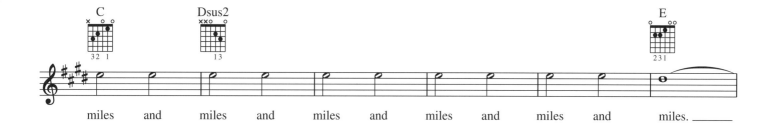

miles and miles and miles and miles and miles and miles. _____

Outro   *Repeat and Fade*

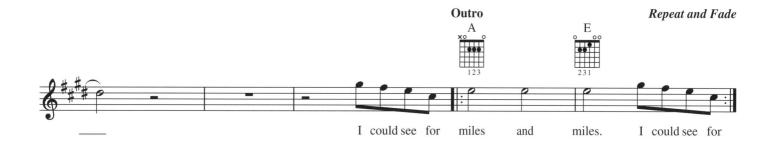

_____ I could see for miles and miles. I could see for

Additional Lyrics

3. You took advantage of my trust in you when I was so far away.
   I saw you holding lots of other guys, and now you have the nerve to say
   That you still want me. Well, that's as maybe,
   But you gotta stand trial, because all the while,

I Fall to Pieces

Words and Music by Hank Cochran and Harlan Howard

Strum Pattern: 3
Pick Pattern: 3

Additional Lyrics

Chorus 2. I fall to pieces each time someone speaks your name.
I fall to pieces. Time only adds to the flame.

Verse 2. You tell me to find someone else to love,
Someone who'll love me too, the way you used to do.
But each time I go out with someone new,
You walk by and I fall to pieces.

I Walk the Line

Words and Music by John R. Cash

Strum Pattern: 4
Pick Pattern: 5

Intro
Moderately Fast

1. I keep a close watch on this heart of mine. ___ I keep my eyes wide o-pen all the
2., 3., 4. *See Additional Lyrics*

time. ___ I keep the ends out for the time that binds. ___ Be-cause you're

1. mine ___ I walk the line. ___ 2. I find it line. ___ 3. As sure as

3. line. ___ 4. You've got a line. ___ 5. I keep a line. ___

Additional Lyrics

2. I find it very easy to be true.
 I find myself alone when each day is through.
 Yes, I'll admit that I'm a fool for you.
 Because you're mine I walk the line.

3. As sure as night is dark and day is light,
 I keep you on my mind both day and night.
 And happiness I've known proves that it's right.

4. You've got a way to keep me on your side.
 You give me cause for love that I can't hide.
 For you I know I'd even try to turn the tide.
 Because you're mine I walk the line.

5. I keep a close watch on this heart of mine.
 I keep my eyes wide open all the time.
 I keep the ends out for the tie that binds.
 Because you're mine I walk the line.

I'm So Excited

Words and Music by Trevor Lawrence, June Pointer, Ruth Pointer and Anita Pointer

Strum Pattern: 4
Pick Pattern: 1

Intro
Strong, Steady Beat

1. To - night, __ to - night __ we're gon -
2. *See Additional Lyrics*
3. *Instrumental*

- na make __ it hap - pen, to - night __ we'll put __ all

oth - er things __ a - side. __ Get in _____ this time __ and

show me some _ af - fec - tion, we're go - in' for __ those

To Coda ⊕

pleas - ures in the night. __ I want to love you, __

feel you, __ wrap my - self a - round __ you. I want to squeeze you, __

Additional Lyrics

We shouldn't even think about tomorrow,
Sweet memories will last a long, long time.
We'll have a good time, baby, don't you worry,
Adn if we're still playin' around, boy, that's just fine.

Luck Be a Lady

from GUYS AND DOLLS

By Frank Loesser

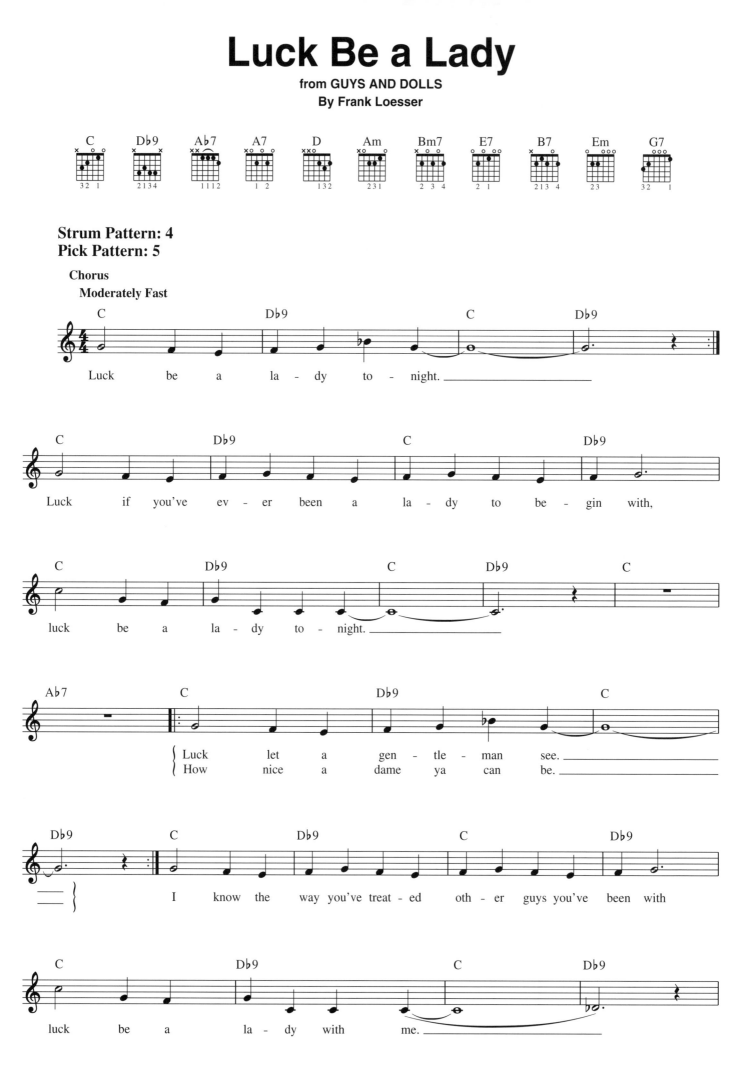

Strum Pattern: 4
Pick Pattern: 5

Chorus
Moderately Fast

Luck be a la-dy to-night.

Luck if you've ev-er been a la-dy to be-gin with,

luck be a la-dy to-night.

Luck let a gen-tle-man see.

How nice a dame ya can be.

I know the way you've treat-ed oth-er guys you've been with

luck be a la-dy with me.

Bridge

A la - dy does - n't leave her
es - cort; _____ it is - n't fair, _____ it is - n't
nice. _____ A la - dy does - n't wan - der all
o - ver the room and blow on some oth - er guy's

Chorus

dice. _____ So let's keep the
                   nev - er get
par - ty po - lite. _____ Stick with me
out of my sight. _____
ba - by I'm the fel - low you came in with. Luck be a
la - dy, luck be a la - dy, luck be a
la - dy to - night. _____

Oh, What a Beautiful Mornin'

from OKLAHOMA!
Lyrics by Oscar Hammerstein II
Music by Richard Rodgers

Strum Pattern: 8
Pick Pattern: 8

Bright Waltz   **Verse**

1. There's a bright gold - en haze on the mead - ow,_____ there's a
2., 3. *See Additional Lyrics*

bright gold - en haze on the mead - ow. _____ The corn is as

high as an el - e - phant's eye, an' it looks like it's

climb - in' clear up to the sky.   Oh, what a beau - ti - ful

morn - in', oh, what a beau - ti - ful day. _____

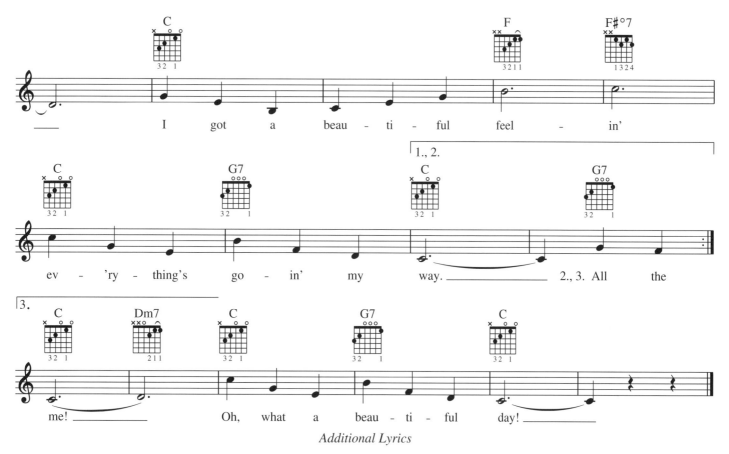

Chords: C, F, F#°7, C, G7, C, G7, C, Dm7, C, G7, C

I got a beau-ti-ful feel-in'

ev-'ry-thing's go-in' my way. 2., 3. All the

3. me! Oh, what a beau-ti-ful day!

Additional Lyrics

2. All the cattle are standin' like statues,
   All the cattle are standin' like statues.
   They don't turn their heads as they see me ride by,
   But a little brown mav'rick is winking her eye.

3. All the sounds of the earth are like music,
   All the sounds of the earth are like music.
   The breeze is so busy, it don't miss a tree
   And an ol' weepin' willer is laughin' at me!

We Are the Champions

Words and Music by Freddie Mercury

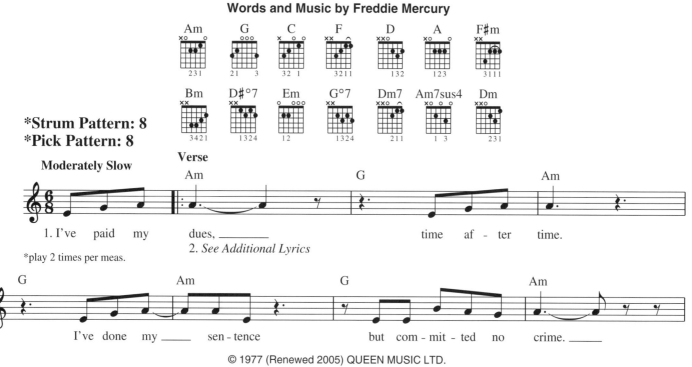

Am, G, C, F, D, A, F#m
Bm, D#°7, Em, G°7, Dm7, Am7sus4, Dm

*Strum Pattern: 8
*Pick Pattern: 8

Moderately Slow

Verse

Am, G, Am

1. I've paid my dues, time af-ter time.

2. *See Additional Lyrics*

*play 2 times per meas.

G, Am, G, Am

I've done my sen-tence but com-mit-ted no crime.

Additional Lyrics

2. I've taken my bows
   And my curtain calls.
   You brought me fame and fortune and ev'rything that goes with it,
   I thank you all.
   But it's been no bed of roses,
   No pleasure cruise.
   I consider it a challenge before the whole human race
   And I ain't gonna lose.

Smoky Mountain Rain

Words and Music by Kye Fleming and Dennis Morgan

Strum Pattern: 1
Pick Pattern: 2

Verse
Moderately

1. I thumbed my way from L. A. back to Knox - ville; I found
2. *See Additional Lyrics*

out those bright lights ain't where I be - long. From a

phone booth in the rain, I called to tell her

I've had a change of dreams, I'm com - ing home; But tears

filled my eyes when I found out she was gone.

Chorus

Smok - y Moun - tain rain, keeps on fall - ing; I keep on call - ing

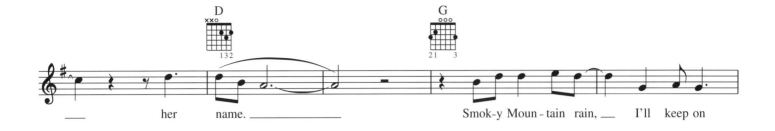

___ her name. _____ Smok-y Moun-tain rain, __ I'll keep on

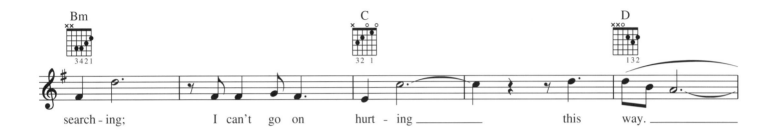

search - ing; I can't go on hurt - ing _____ this way. _____

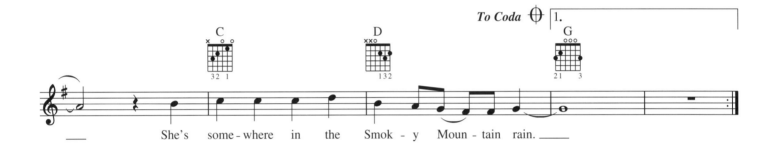

To Coda ⊕ | 1.

___ She's some - where in the Smok- y Moun - tain rain. _____

2.

Bridge

___ I can't blame her for let - ting go;

D.S. al Coda

a wom - an needs some - one warm _____ to hold. __ I feel the rain run - ning

down __ my face; __ I'll find her no mat - ter what it takes. _____

176

⊕ *Coda*

Chorus

Smok-y Moun-tain rain __ keeps on fall-ing;

I keep on call-ing __ her name. __

Smok-y Moun-tain rain, __ I'll keep on search-ing; I can't go on

hurt-ing __ this way. __ She's

Repeat and Fade

some-where in the Smok-y Moun-tain rain. __

Additional Lyrics

2. I waved a diesel down outsde a cafe;
   He said that he was going as far as Gatlinburg.
   I climbed up in the cab, all wet and cold and lonely;
   I wiped my eyes and told him about her.
   I've got to find her, can you make these big wheels burn?

Son-of-a-Preacher Man

Words and Music by John Hurley and Ronnie Wilkins

Strum Pattern: 2
Pick Pattern: 4

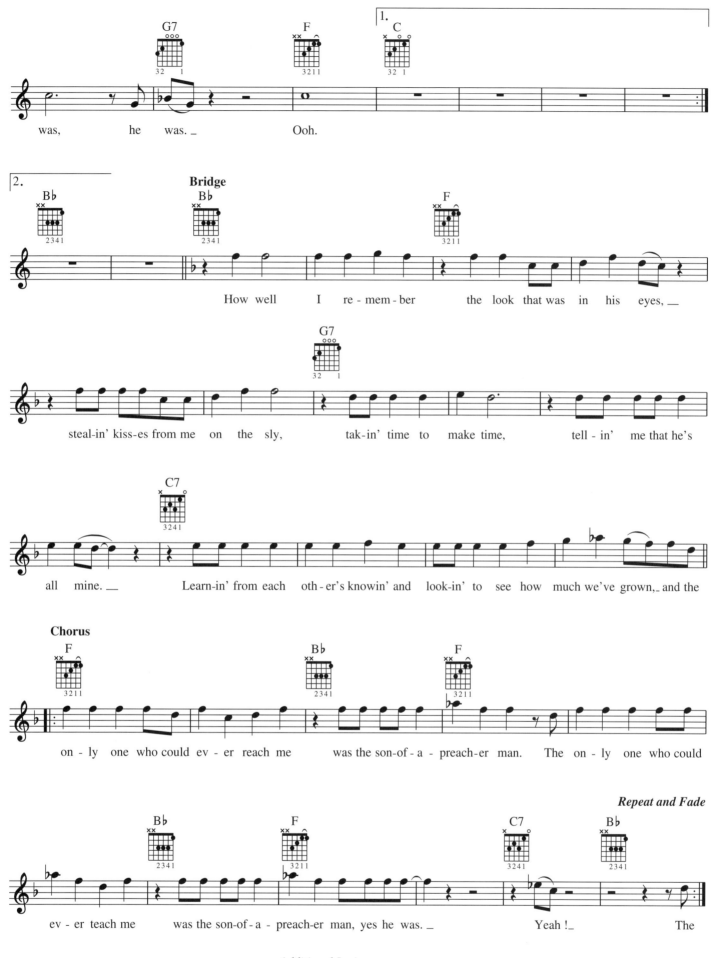

Additional Lyrics

2. Being good isn't always easy no matter how I try.
When he started sweet talkin' to me he'd come and tell me ev'rything is alright;
Kiss and tell me ev'rything is alright, and "Can I sneak away again tonight."
Lord knows to my surprise,

What's My Age Again?

Words and Music by Tom De Longe and Mark Hoppus

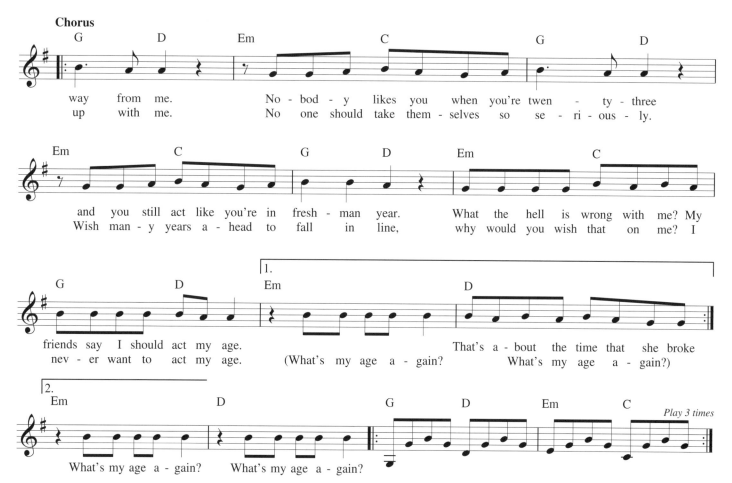

And that's a - bout the time she walked a -

Chorus

way from me.   No - bod - y likes you when you're twen - ty - three
up with me.   No one should take them - selves so se - ri - ous - ly.

and you still act like you're in fresh - man year.   What the hell is wrong with me? My
Wish man - y years a - head to fall in line,   why would you wish that on me? I

friends say I should act my age.   That's a - bout the time that she broke
nev - er want to act my age.   (What's my age a - gain?   What's my age a - gain?)

What's my age a - gain?   What's my age a - gain?   *Play 3 times*

What's my age a - gain? ___

When You Say Nothing at All

Words and Music by Don Schlitz and Paul Overstreet

Strum Pattern: 1
Pick Pattern: 2

touch of your hand ___ says you'll catch ___ me if ev - er I fall. ___

To Coda ⊕ |1.

Now you say it best ___ when you say noth-ing at all. ___

|2.

when you say noth - ing at all. ___

Interlude

D.S. al Coda

___ The

⊕ *Coda*

when you say noth-ing at all. ___

rit.

Additional Lyrics

2. All day long I can hear people talking out loud,
   But when you hold me near you drown out the crowd.
   Old mister Webster could never define
   What's being said between your heart and mine.

Come Fly with Me

Words by Sammy Cahn
Music by James Van Heusen

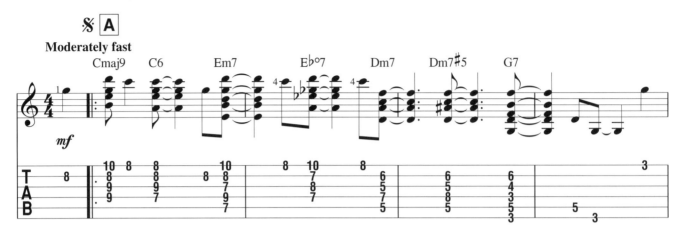

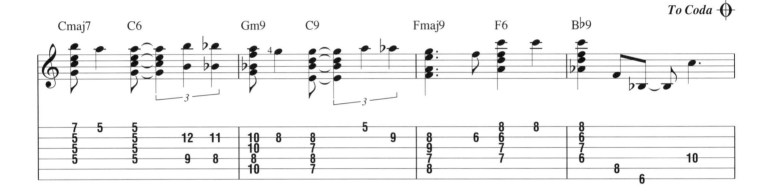

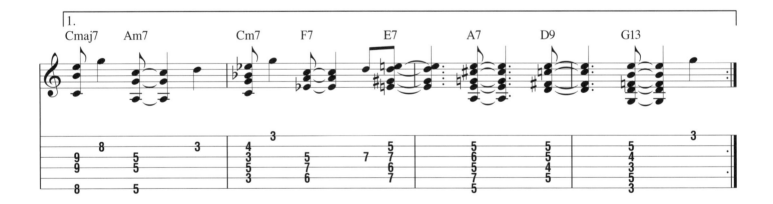

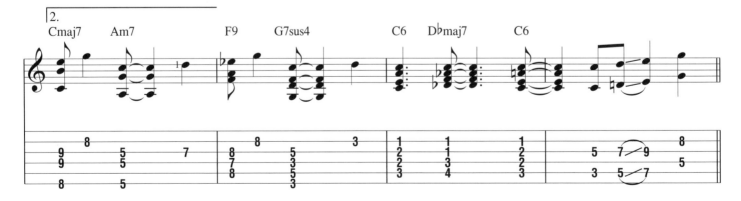

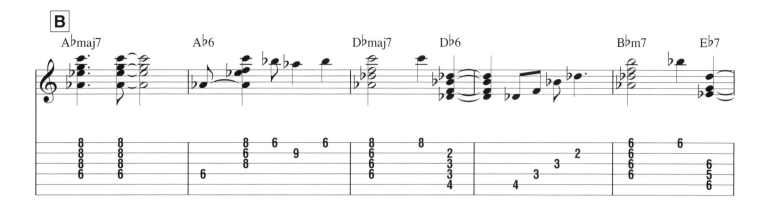

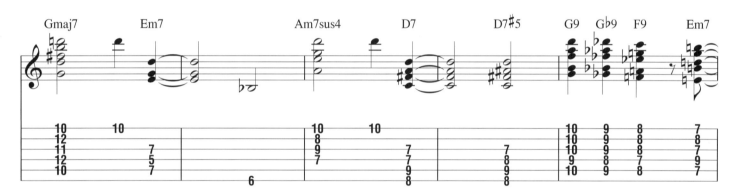

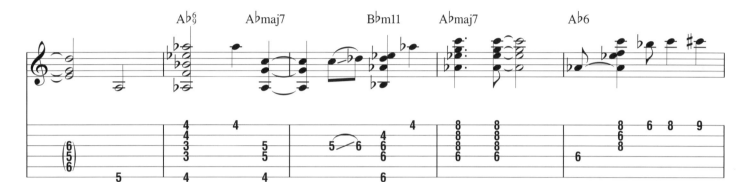

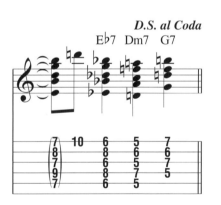

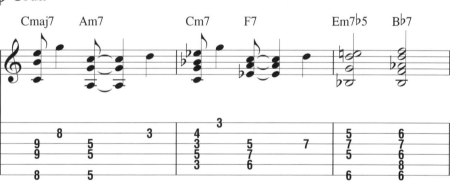

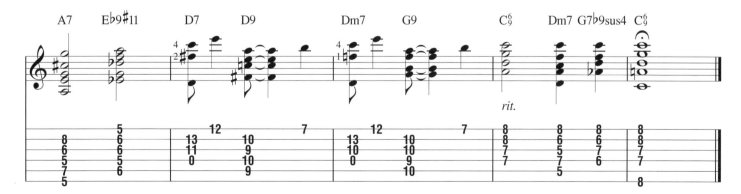

Feliz Navidad

Music and Lyrics by José Feliciano

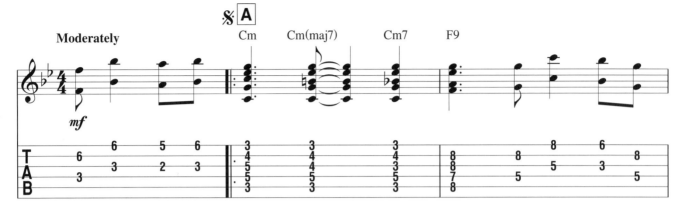

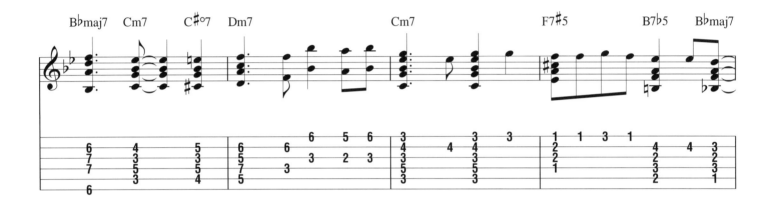

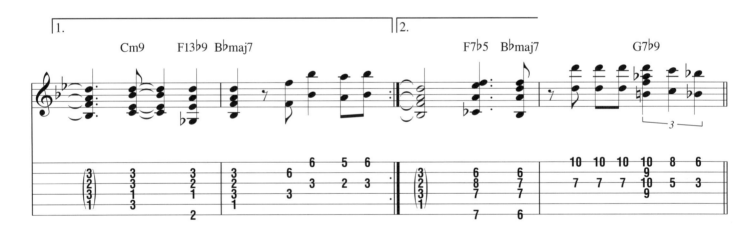

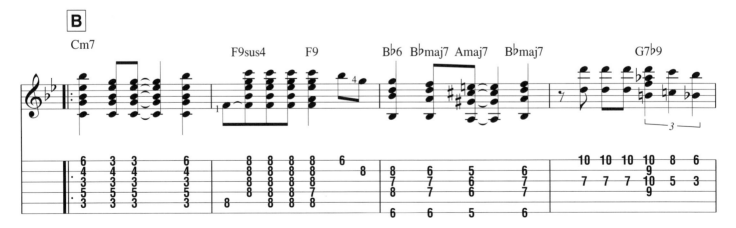

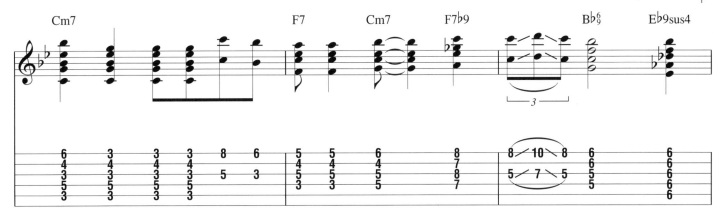

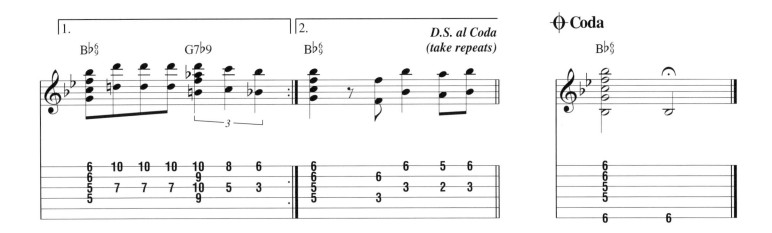

A Fine Romance

from SWING TIME

Words by Dorothy Fields
Music by Jerome Kern

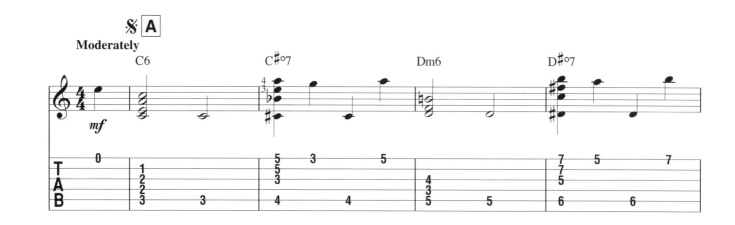

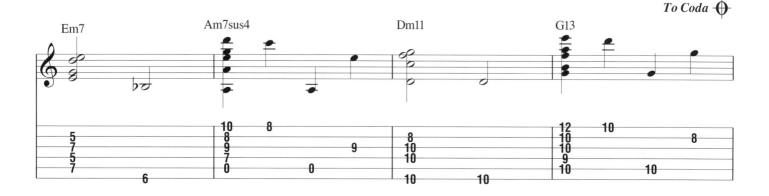

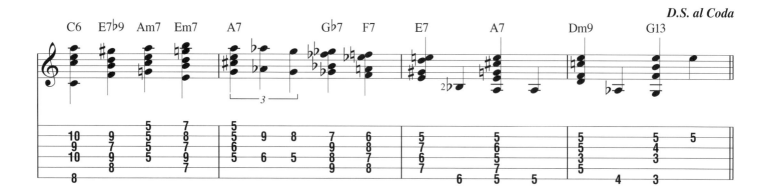

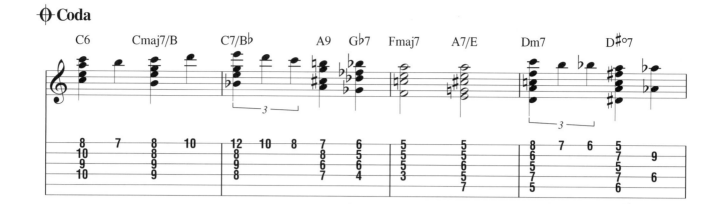

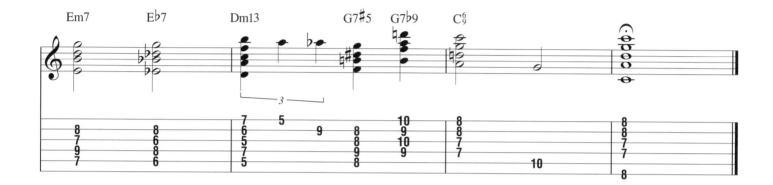

I'll Be Seeing You

from RIGHT THIS WAY

Written by Irving Kahal and Sammy Fain

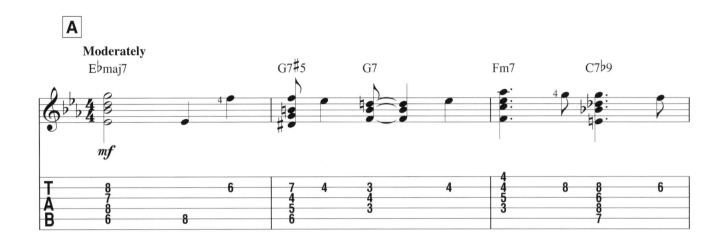

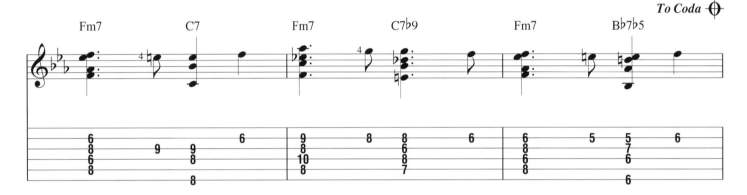

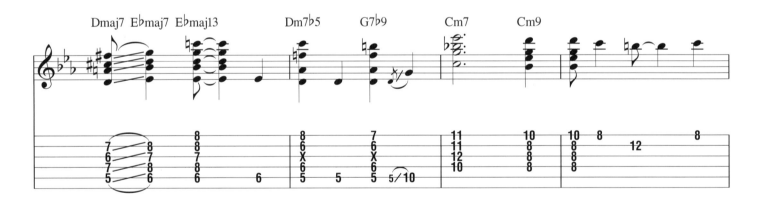

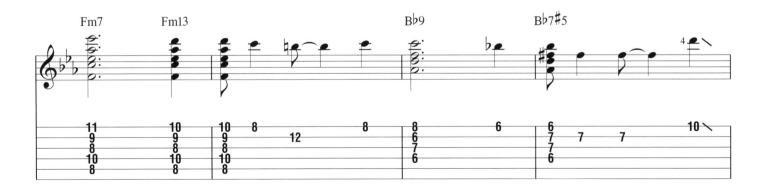

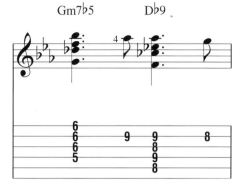

Coda

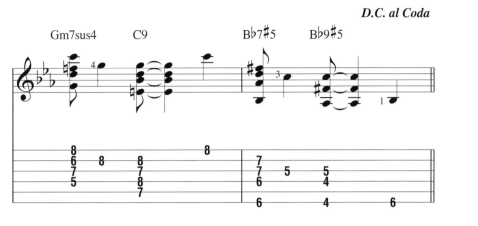

D.C. al Coda

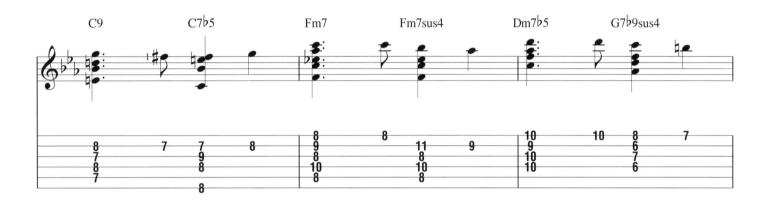

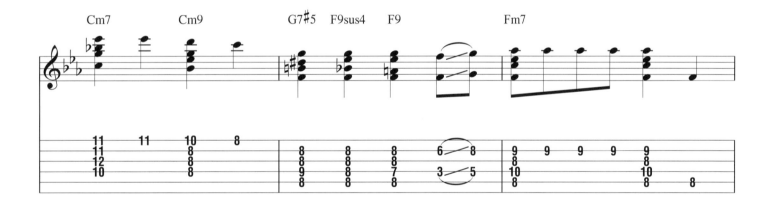

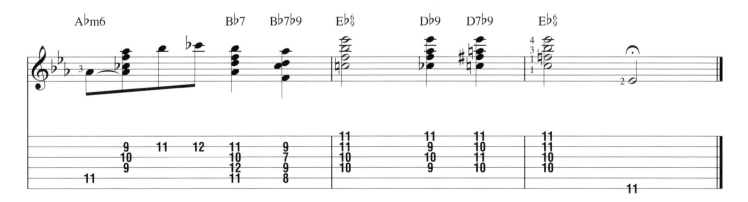

Witchcraft

Music by Cy Coleman
Lyrics by Carolyn Leigh

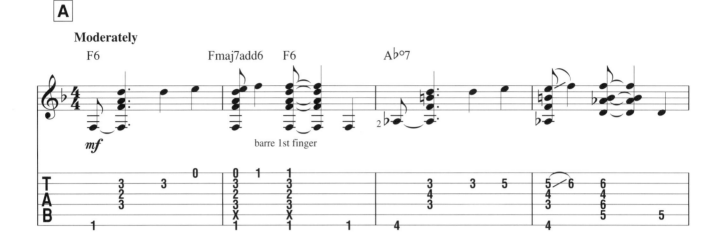

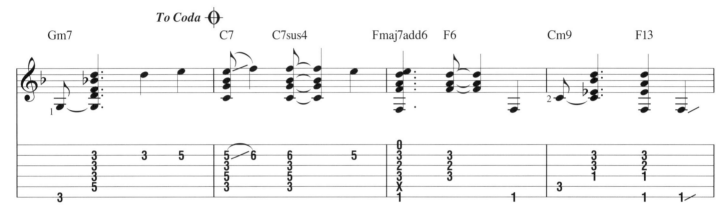

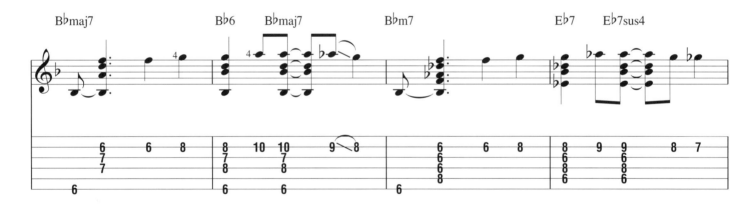

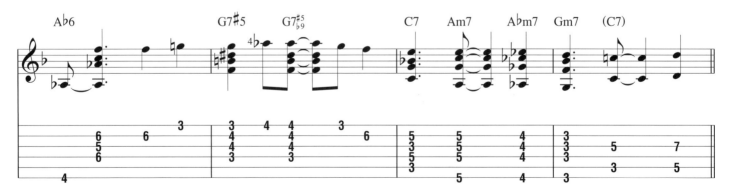

B

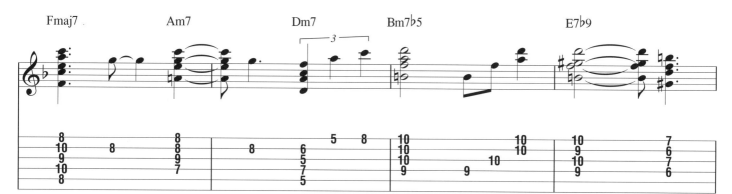

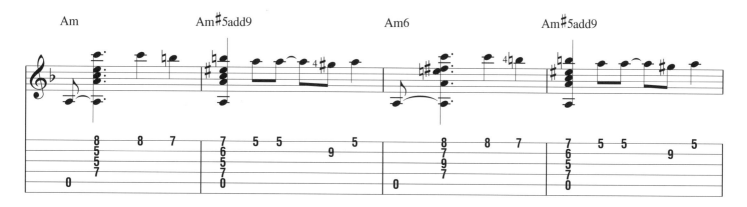

D.C. al Coda

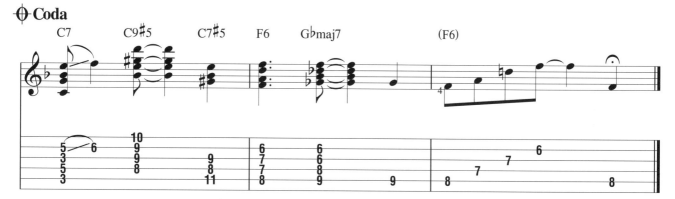

Capricho Árabe

Written by Francisco Tárrega

Tuning:
(low to high) D–A–D–G–B–B

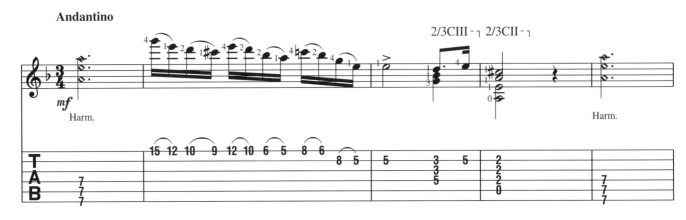

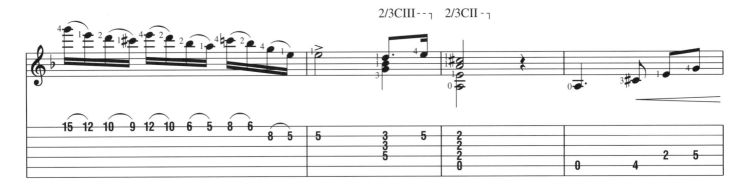

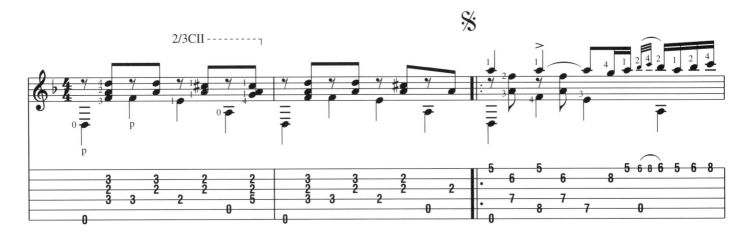

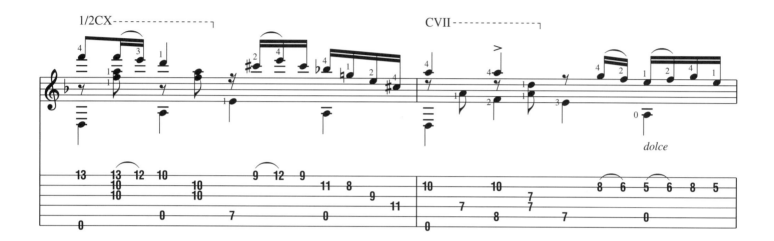

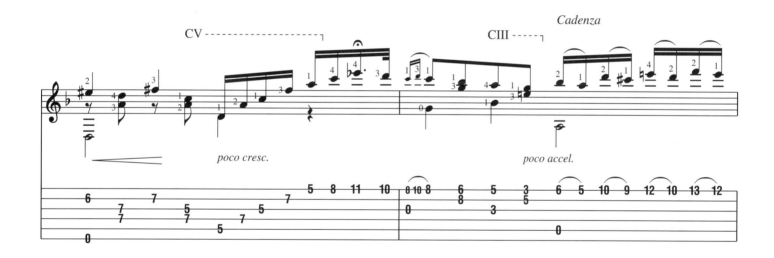

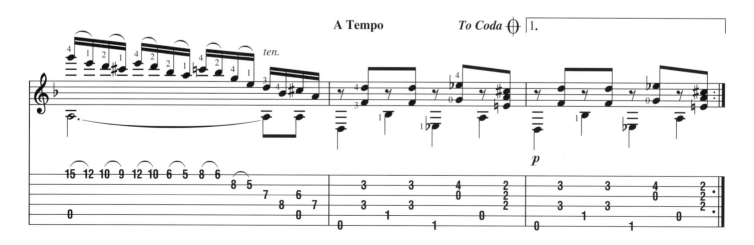

2.

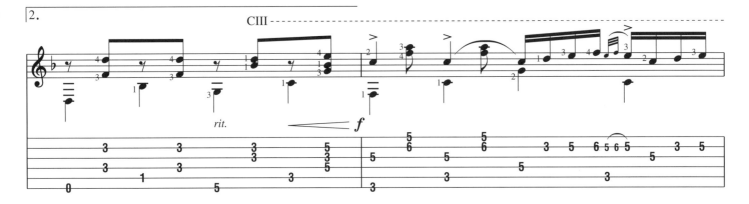

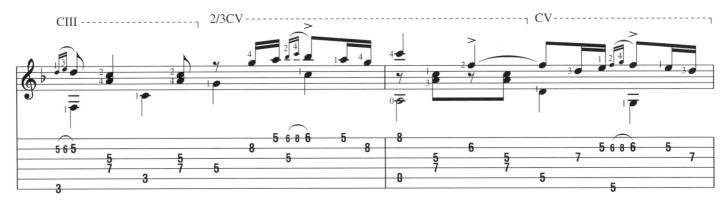

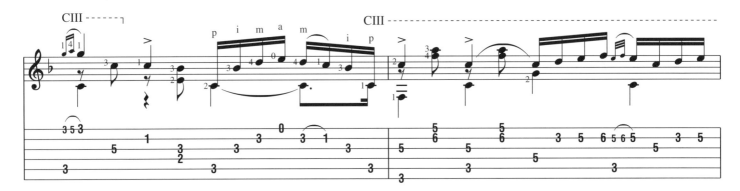

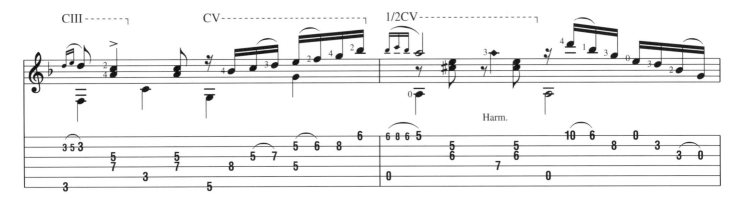

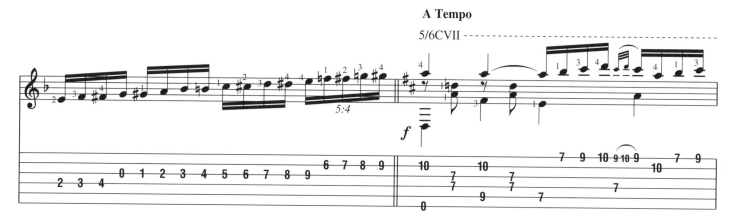

A Tempo

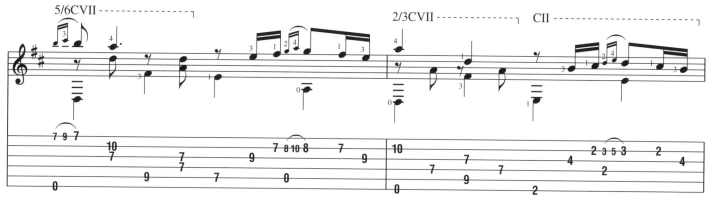

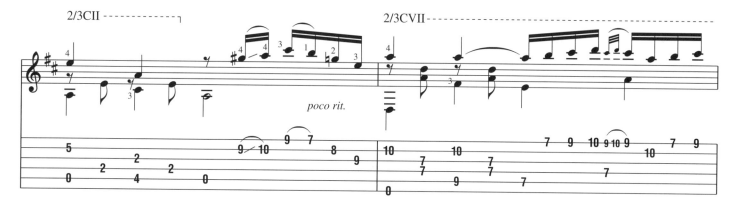

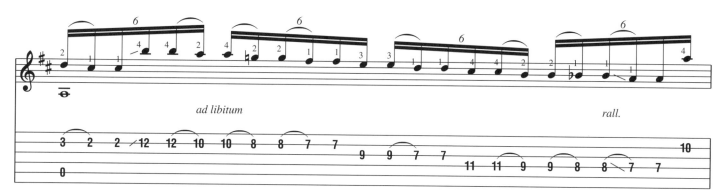

A Tempo

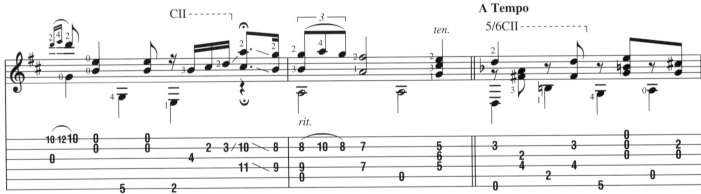

D.S. al Coda

Coda

Españoleta

By Gaspar Sanz

Minuet in G

By Johann Sebastian Bach

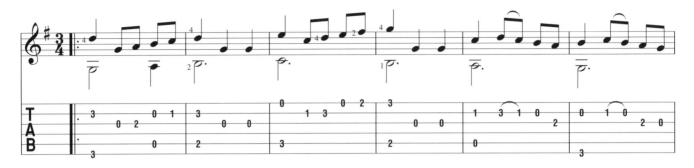

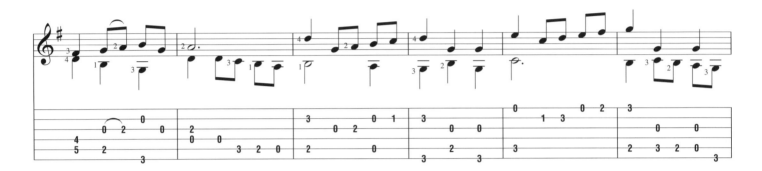

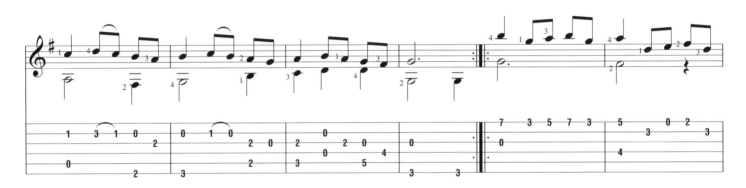

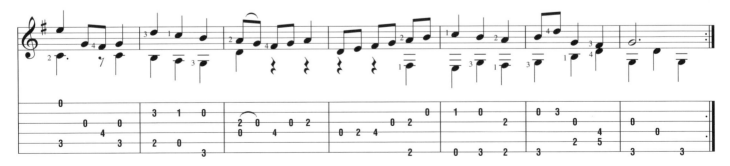

Study

Op. 60, No. 7

By Matteo Carcassi

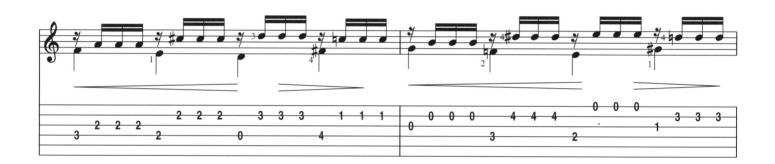

Piano Sonata No. 14 In C♯ Minor

("Moonlight Sonata")
Op. 27 No. 2 First Movement Theme
By Ludwig van Beethoven

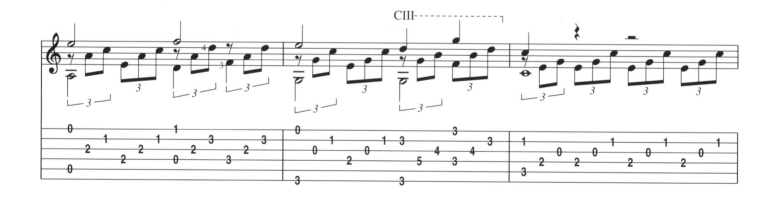

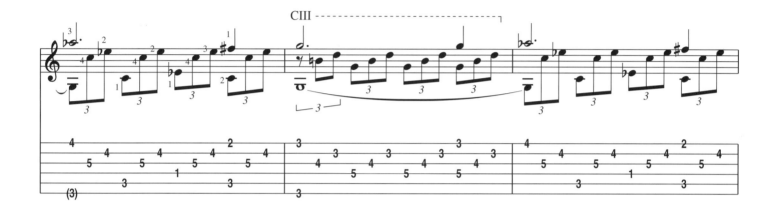

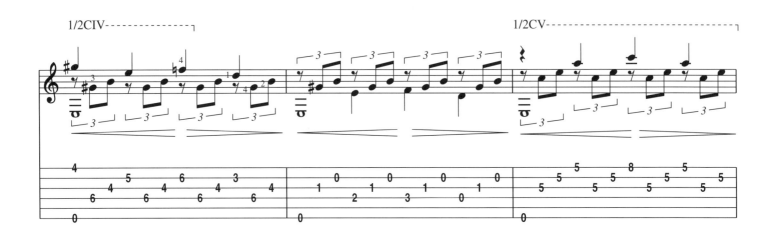

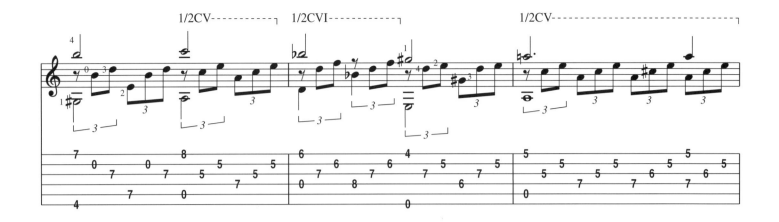

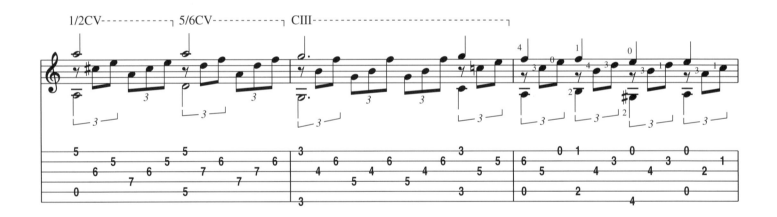

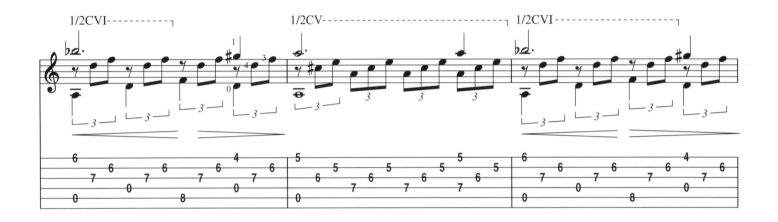

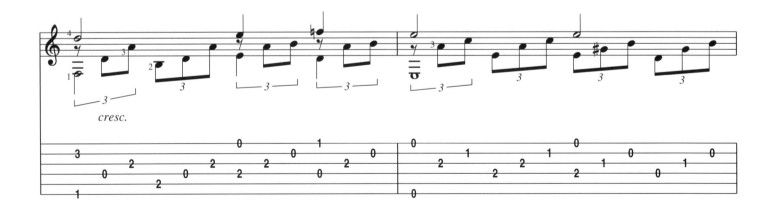

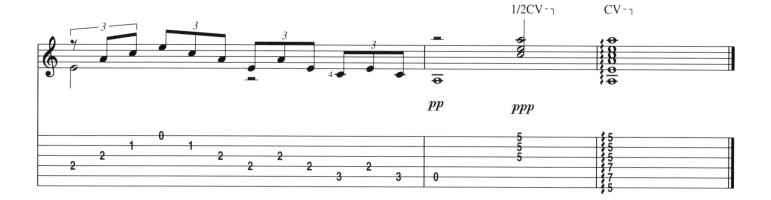

Blue Eyes Crying in the Rain

Words and Music by Fred Rose

Drop D tuning:
(low to high) D–A–D–G–B–E

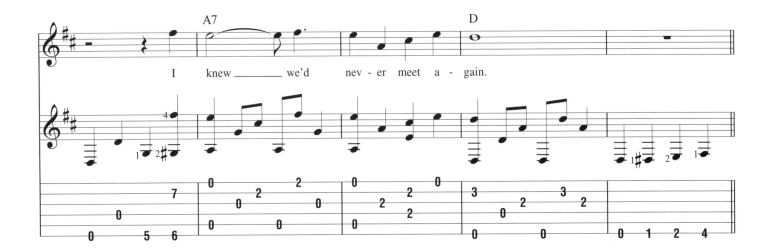

Chorus

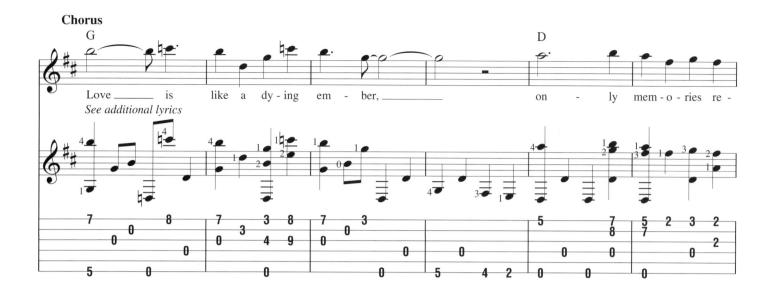

Love _____ is like a dy - ing em - ber, _____ on - ly mem - o - ries re -

See additional lyrics

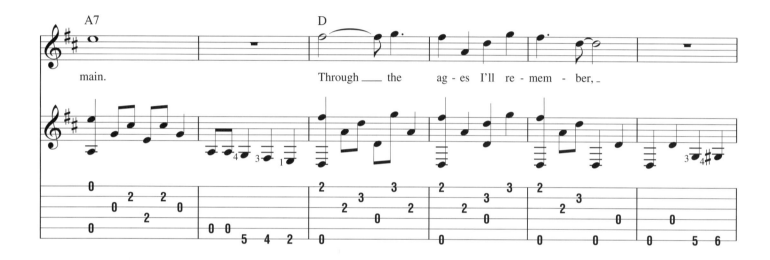

main. Through ____ the ag - es I'll re - mem - ber, _

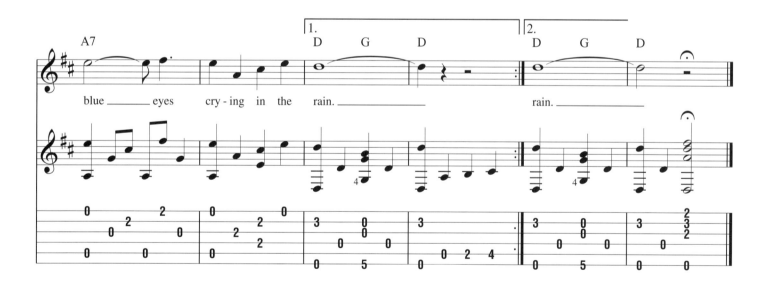

blue _____ eyes cry - ing in the rain. _____ rain. _____

Additional Lyrics

2. Now my hair has turned to silver.
   All my life I've loved in vain.
   I can see her star in heaven,
   Blue eyes crying in the rain.

Chorus Someday when we meet up yonder,
   We'll stroll hand in hand again
   In a land that knows no parting,
   Blue eyes crying in the rain.

Every Rose Has Its Thorn

Words and Music by Bobby Dall, Brett Michaels, Bruce Johannesson and Rikki Rockett

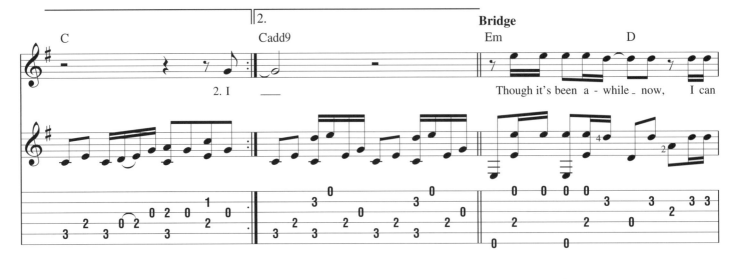

2.

Bridge

2. I ___

Though it's been a - while ___ now, I can

still feel so much pain. ___

Like the knife that cuts ___ you, the wound heals, but the scar, that scar re-

Interlude

mains.

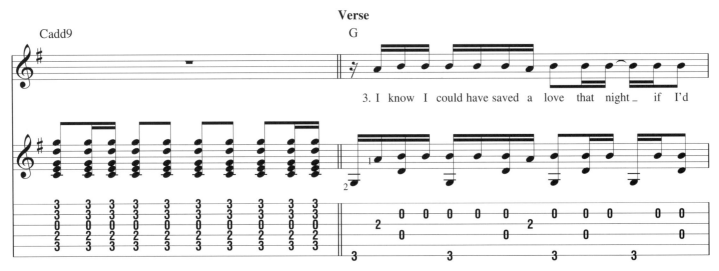

Verse

3. I know I could have saved a love that night ___ if I'd

214

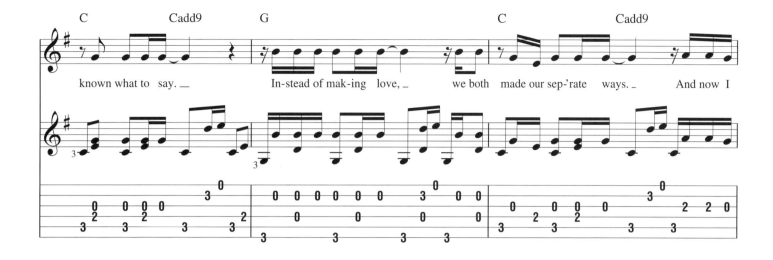

known what to say. _   In-stead of mak-ing love, _   we both made our sep-'rate ways. _   And now I

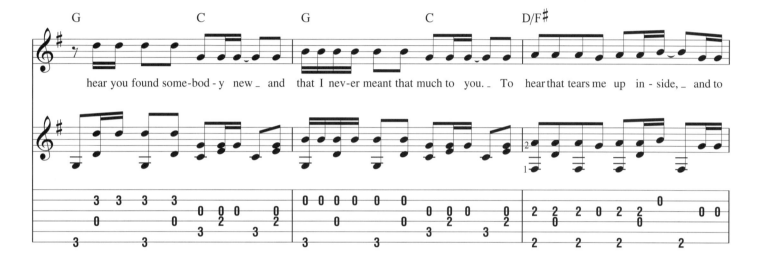

hear you found some-bod - y new _ and that I nev-er meant that much to you. _ To   hear that tears me up in - side, _ and to

𝄋 **Coda**

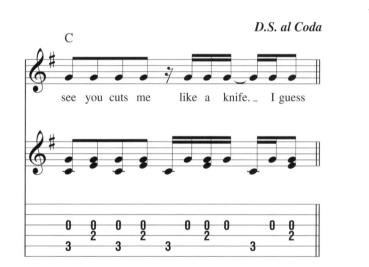

D.S. al Coda

see you cuts me   like a knife. _ I guess

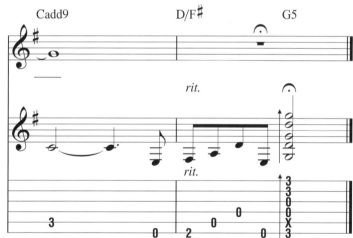

rit.

Additional Lyrics

2. I listen to our fav'rite song
   Playin' on the radio.
   Hear the D.J. say,
   "Love's a game of easy come and easy go."
   But, I wonder, does he know?
   Has he ever felt like this?
   And I know that you'd be right here now
   If I coulda let you know somehow.
   I guess...

Fields of Gold

Music and Lyrics by Sting

Verse
Moderately

1. You'll re - mem-ber me, — when the west wind moves, — up - on the fields — of bar -
3. *See additional lyrics*

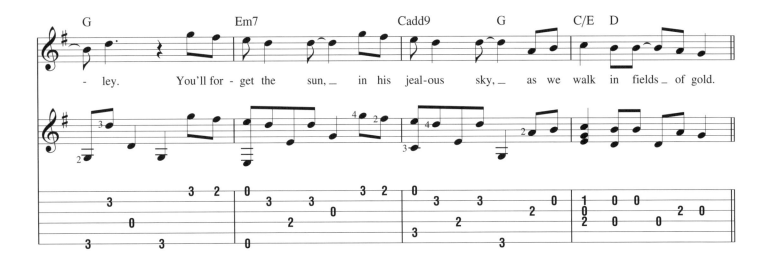

- ley. You'll for - get the sun, — in his jeal-ous sky, — as we walk in fields — of gold.

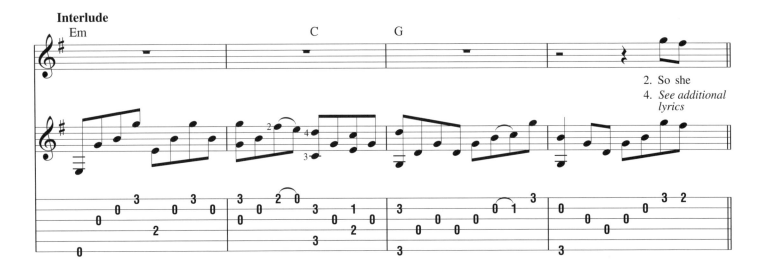

Interlude

2. So she
4. *See additional lyrics*

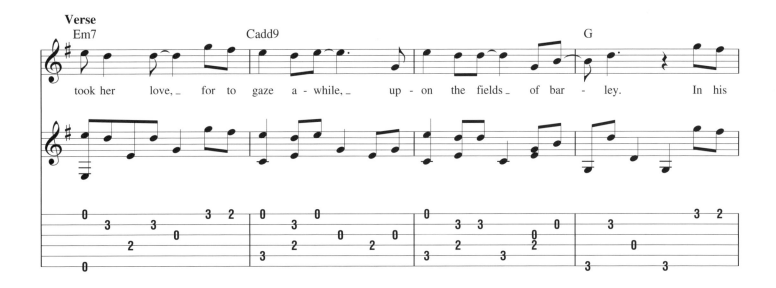

took her love, _ for to gaze a - while, _ up - on the fields _ of bar - ley. In his

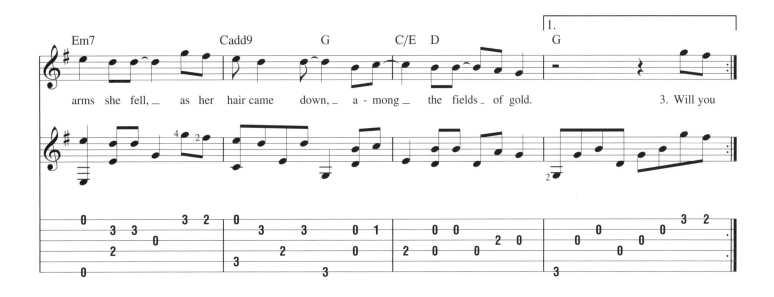

arms she fell, _ as her hair came down, _ a - mong _ the fields _ of gold.   3. Will you

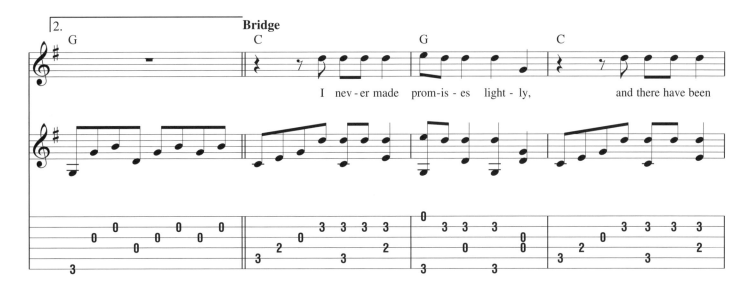

I nev - er made prom - is - es light - ly,   and there have been

some that I've bro - ken. But I swear, _ in the days still left, we'll walk _ in fields _ of gold.

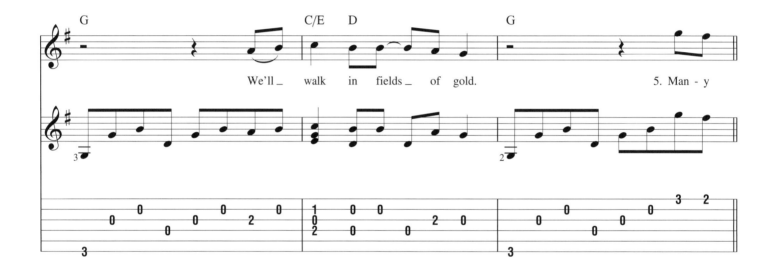

We'll _ walk in fields _ of gold. 5. Man - y

Verse

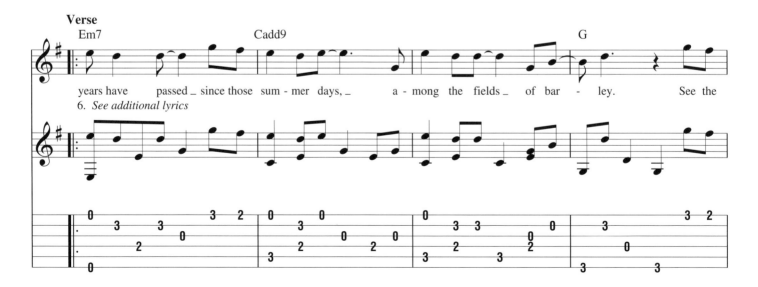

years have passed _ since those sum - mer days, _ a - mong the fields _ of bar - ley. See the
6. *See additional lyrics*

Additional Lyrics

3. Will you stay with me, will you be my love,
   Among the fields of barley?
   We'll forget the sun in his jealous sky,
   As we lie in fields of gold.

4. See the west wind move, like a lover so,
   Upon the fields of barley.
   Feel her body rise, when you kiss her mouth
   Among the fields of gold.

6. You'll remember me, when the west wind moves,
   Upon the fields of barley.
   You can tell the sun, in his jealous sky,
   When we walked in fields of gold,
   When we walked in fields of gold,
   When we walked in fields of gold.

I've Grown Accustomed to Her Face

from MY FAIR LADY

Words by Alan Jay Lerner
Music by Frederick Loewe

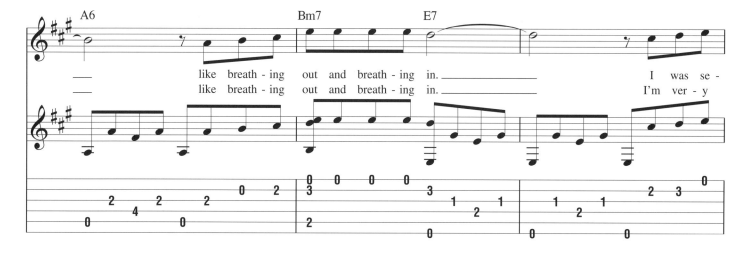

like breath - ing out and breath - ing in. _____ I was se -
like breath - ing out and breath - ing in. _____ I'm ver - y

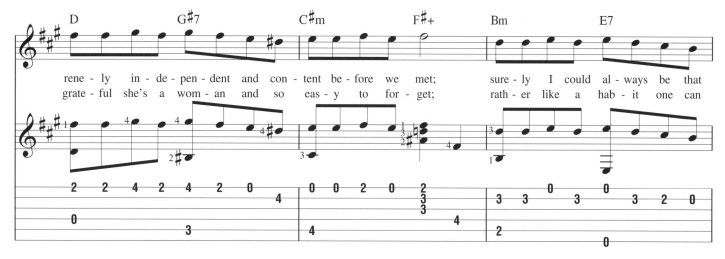

rene - ly in - de - pen - dent and con - tent be - fore we met; sure - ly I could al - ways be that
grate - ful she's a wom - an and so eas - y to for - get; rath - er like a hab - it one can

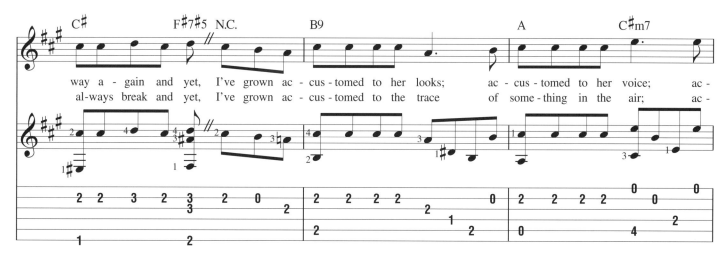

way a - gain and yet, I've grown ac - cus - tomed to her looks; ac - cus - tomed to her voice; ac -
al - ways break and yet, I've grown ac - cus - tomed to the trace of some - thing in the air; ac -

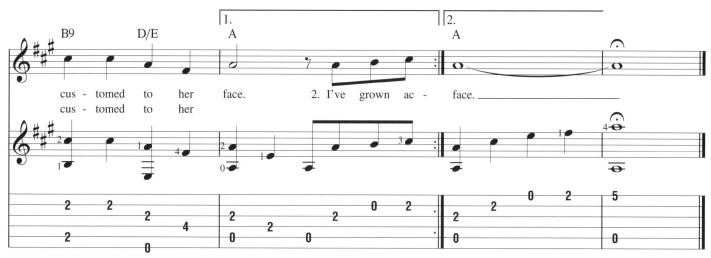

cus - tomed to her face. 2. I've grown ac - face. _____
cus - tomed to her

Rainy Days and Mondays

Lyrics by Paul Williams
Music by Roger Nichols

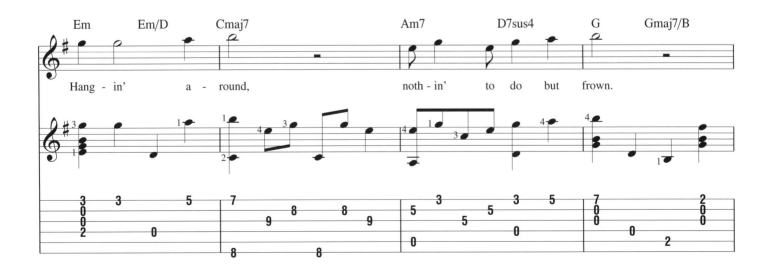

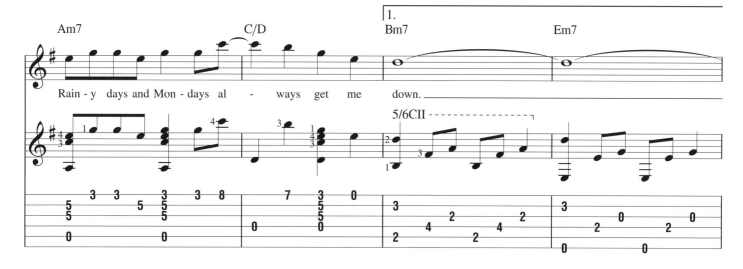

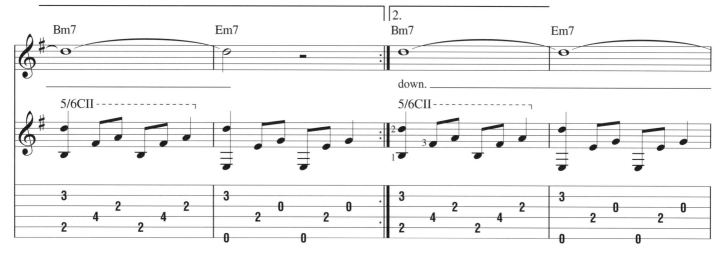

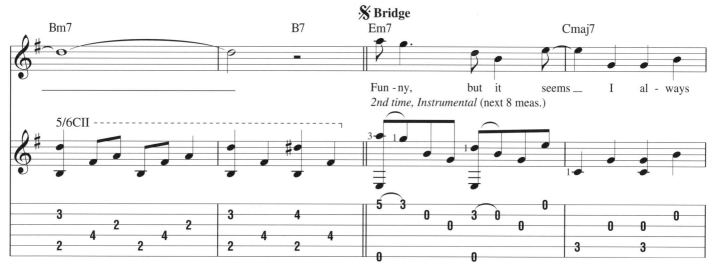

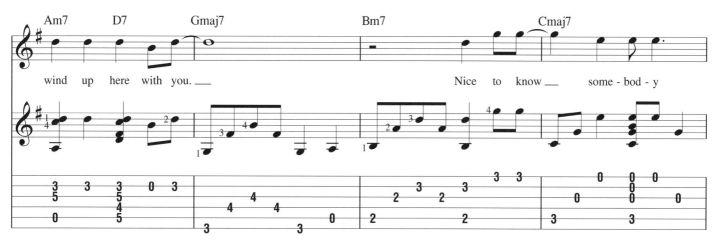

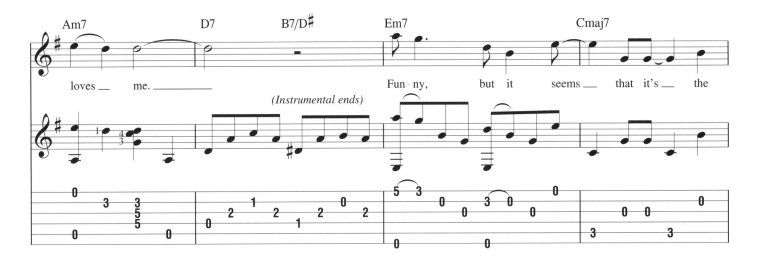

loves __ me. __ *(Instrumental ends)* Fun - ny, but it seems __ that it's __ the

on - ly thing to do, ___ run and find the one __ who

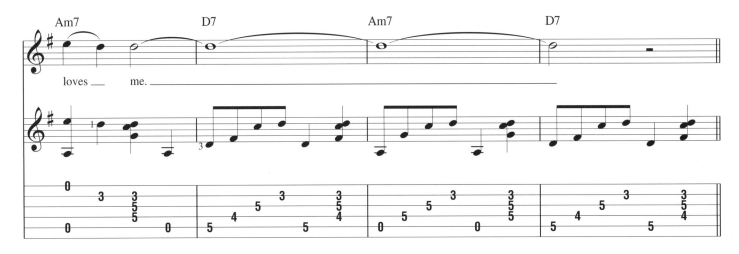

loves __ me. ___

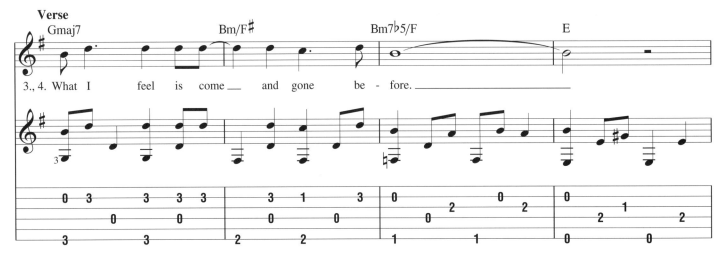

3., 4. What I feel is come __ and gone be - fore. ___

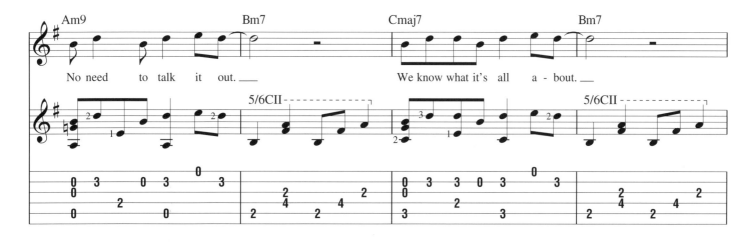

No need to talk it out. ___ We know what it's all a-bout. ___

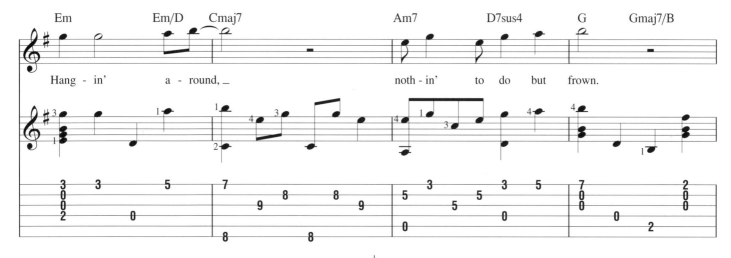

Hang-in' a-round, ___ noth-in' to do but frown.

To Coda ⊕

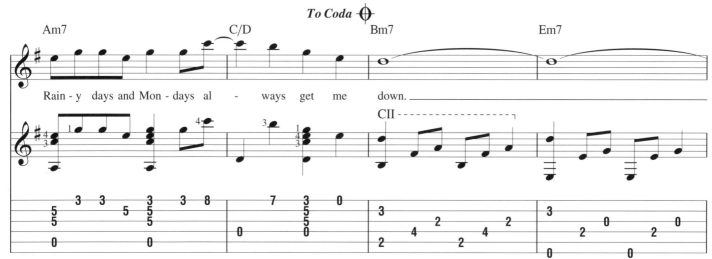

Rain - y days and Mon - days al - ways get me down. _____

⊕ **Coda**

D.S. al Coda

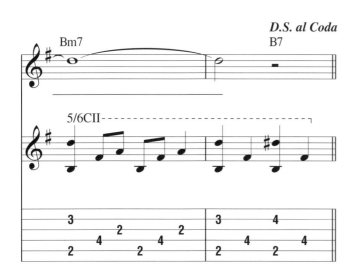

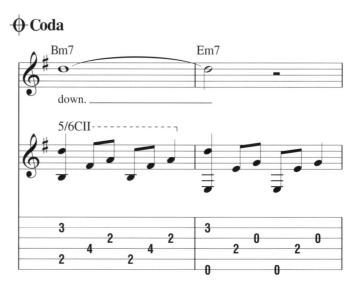

down. _____

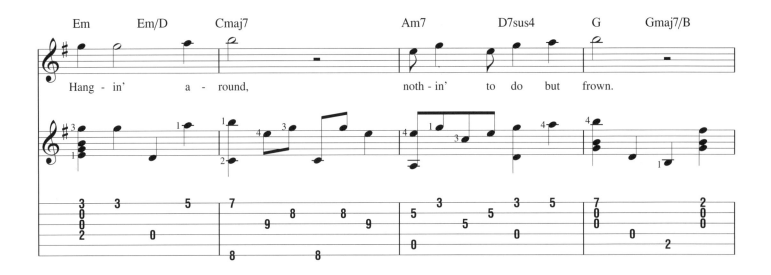

Hang - in' a - round, noth - in' to do but frown.

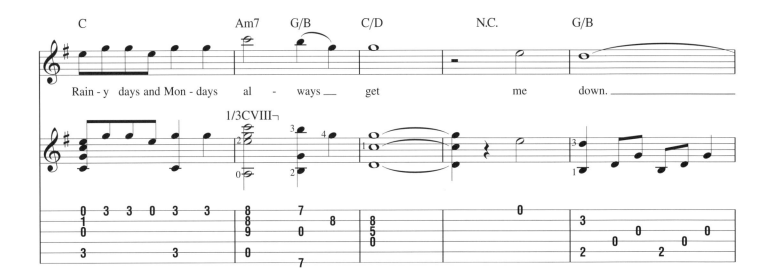

Rain - y days and Mon - days al - ways __ get me down. _____

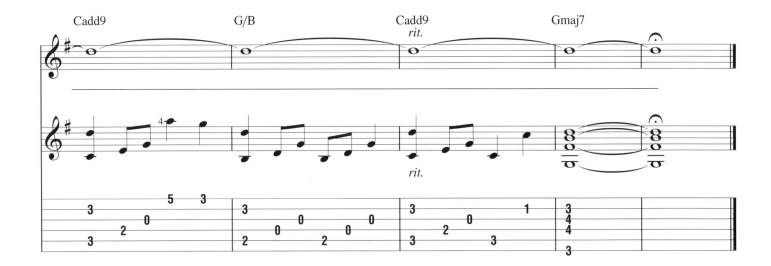

Additional Lyrics

2. What I've got they used to call the blues.
   Nothin' is really wrong, feelin' like I don't belong.
   Walkin' around, some kind of lonely clown.
   Rainy days and Mondays always get me down.

Beautiful Girls

Words and Music by David Lee Roth, Edward Van Halen, Alex Van Halen and Michael Anthony

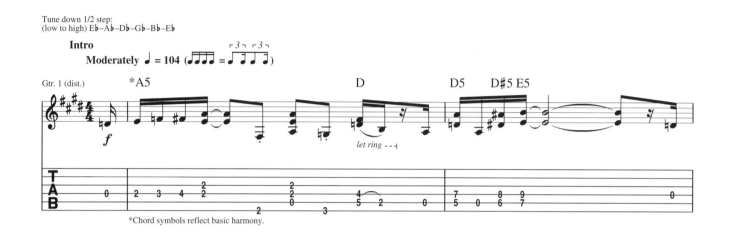

*Chord symbols reflect basic harmony.

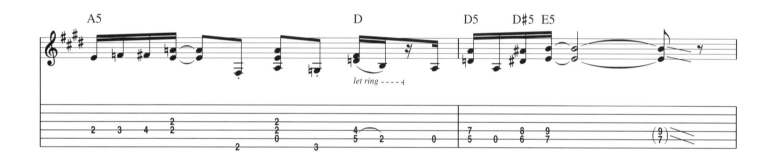

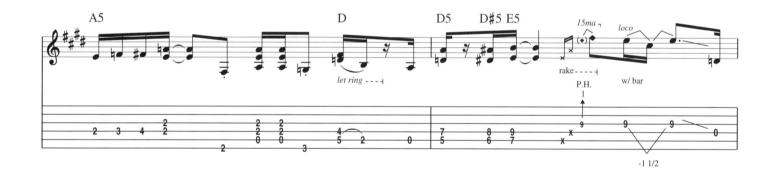

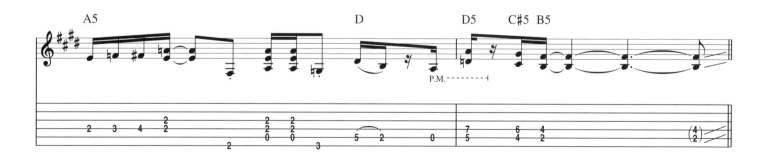

Best of You

Words and Music by Dave Grohl, Taylor Hawkins, Chris Shiflett and Nate Mendel

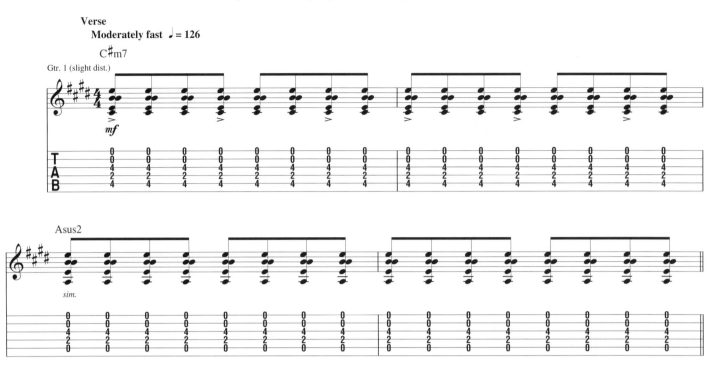

B.Y.O.B.

Words and Music by Daron Malakian and Serj Tankian

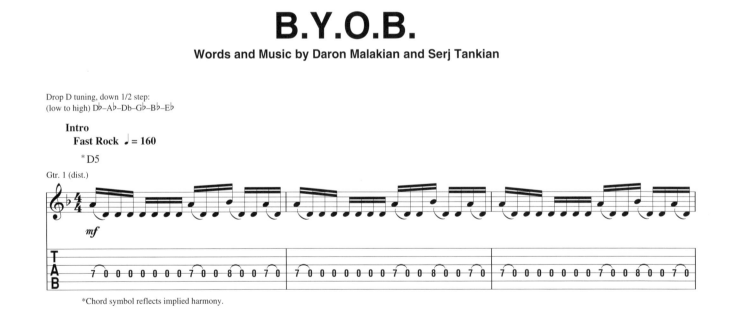

*Chord symbol reflects implied harmony.

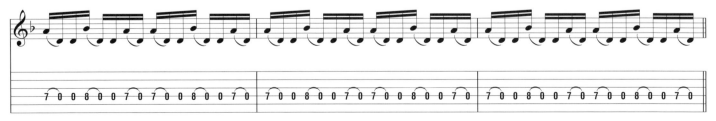

Cheap Sunglasses

Words and Music by Billy F Gibbons, Dusty Hill and Frank Beard

Intro
Moderately ♩ = 96

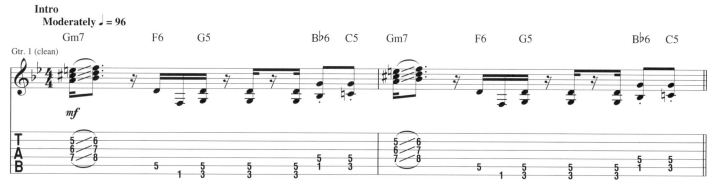

Dancing with Myself

Words and Music by Billy Idol and Tony James

Intro
Fast Rock ♩ = 174

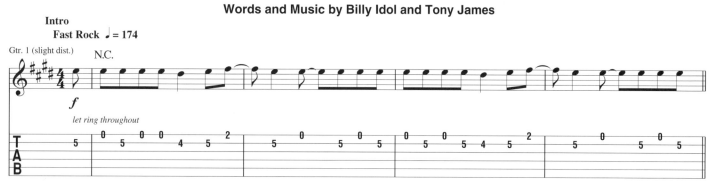

Hurts So Good

Words and Music by John Mellencamp and George Green

Intro
Moderately ♩ = 126

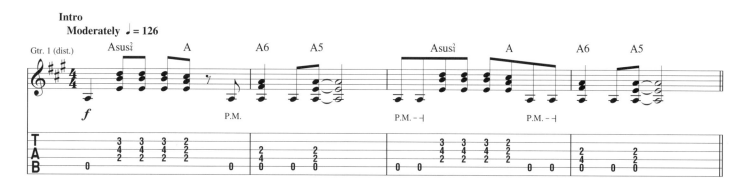

I Hate Myself for Loving You

Words and Music by Desmond Child and Joan Jett

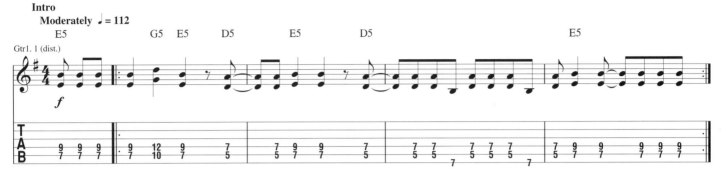

No More Mr. Nice Guy

Words and Music by Alice Cooper and Michael Bruce

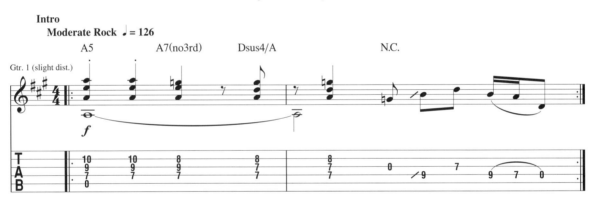

Rock of Ages

Words and Music by Joe Elliott, Richard Savage, Richard Allen, Steve Clark, Peter Willis and Robert Lange

No Rain

Words and Music by Blind Melon

Shine

Words and Music by Ed Roland

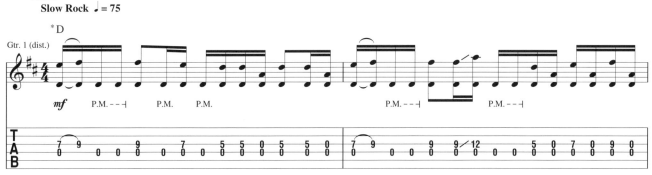

*Chord symbols reflect implied tonality.

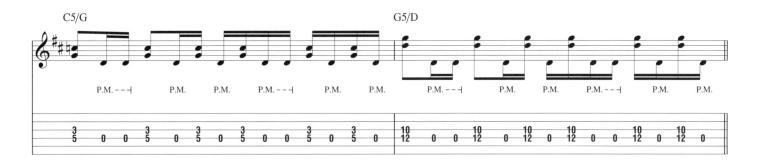

Nothin' but a Good Time

Words and Music by Bobby Dall, Brett Michaels, Bruce Johannesson and Rikki Rockett

Tune down 1/2 step:
(low to high) Eb–Ab–Db–Gb–Bb–Eb

Intro
Moderate Rock ♩ = 132

Secret Agent Man

from the Television Series

Words and Music by P.F. Sloan and Steve Barri

Intro
Fast Rock ♩ = 160
N.C.(Em)

Gtr. 1 (fuzz)

Slide

Words and Music by John Rzeznik

*Tuning
(low to high) D#-A#-D#-G#-D#-D#

*All music is notated one half step lower than actual sounding pitch for ease of reading.

Smokestack Lightning

Words and Music by Chester Burnett

Too Rolling Stoned

Words and Music by Robin Trower

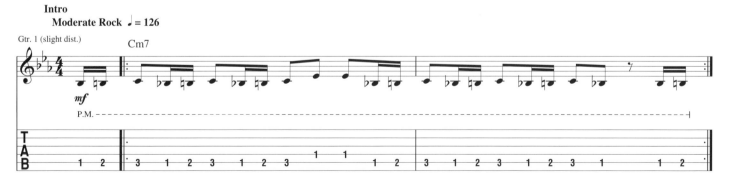

Up Around the Bend

Words and Music by John Fogerty

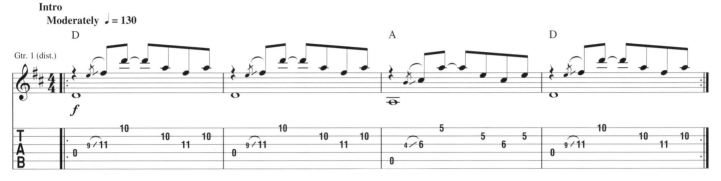

Wang Dang Doodle

Written by Willie Dixon

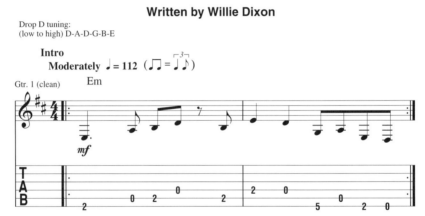

We Gotta Get out of This Place

Words and Music by Barry Mann and Cynthia Weil

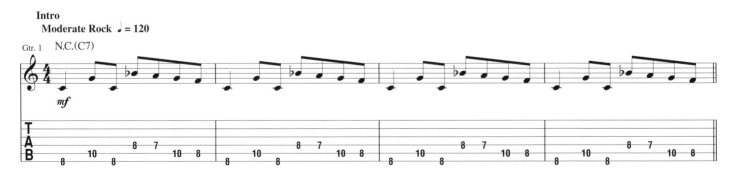

Windy

Words and Music by Ruthann Friedman

Zero

Words and Music by Billy Corgan

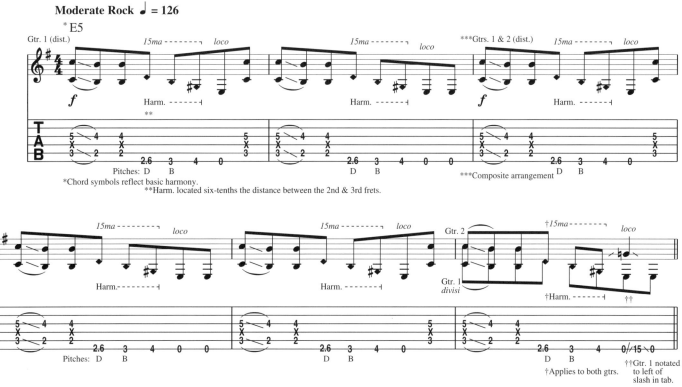

Guitar Notation Legend

Guitar music can be notated three different ways: on a *musical staff*, in *tablature*, and in *rhythm slashes*.

RHYTHM SLASHES are written above the staff. Strum chords in the rhythm indicated. Use the chord diagrams found at the top of the first page of the transcription for the appropriate chord voicings. Round noteheads indicate single notes.

THE MUSICAL STAFF shows pitches and rhythms and is divided by bar lines into measures. Pitches are named after the first seven letters of the alphabet.

TABLATURE graphically represents the guitar fingerboard. Each horizontal line represents a string, and each number represents a fret.

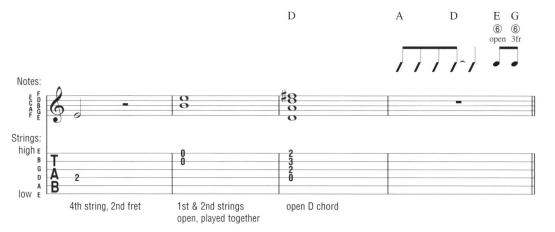

4th string, 2nd fret

1st & 2nd strings open, played together

open D chord

Definitions for Special Guitar Notation

HALF-STEP BEND: Strike the note and bend up 1/2 step.

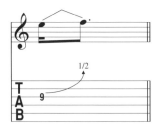

WHOLE-STEP BEND: Strike the note and bend up one step.

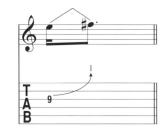

GRACE NOTE BEND: Strike the note and immediately bend up as indicated.

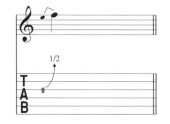

SLIGHT (MICROTONE) BEND: Strike the note and bend up 1/4 step.

BEND AND RELEASE: Strike the note and bend up as indicated, then release back to the original note. Only the first note is struck.

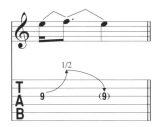

PRE-BEND: Bend the note as indicated, then strike it.

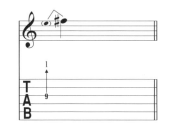

PRE-BEND AND RELEASE: Bend the note as indicated. Strike it and release the bend back to the original note.

UNISON BEND: Strike the two notes simultaneously and bend the lower note up to the pitch of the higher.

VIBRATO: The string is vibrated by rapidly bending and releasing the note with the fretting hand.

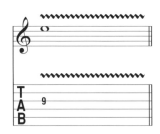

WIDE VIBRATO: The pitch is varied to a greater degree by vibrating with the fretting hand.

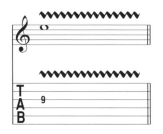

HAMMER-ON: Strike the first (lower) note with one finger, then sound the higher note (on the same string) with another finger by fretting it without picking.

PULL-OFF: Place both fingers on the notes to be sounded. Strike the first note and without picking, pull the finger off to sound the second (lower) note.

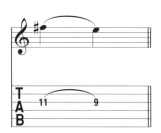

LEGATO SLIDE: Strike the first note and then slide the same fret-hand finger up or down to the second note. The second note is not struck.

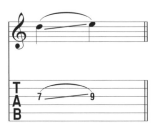

SHIFT SLIDE: Same as legato slide, except the second note is struck.

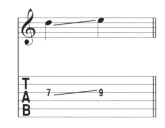

TRILL: Very rapidly alternate between the notes indicated by continuously hammering on and pulling off.

TAPPING: Hammer ("tap") the fret indicated with the pick-hand index or middle finger and pull off to the note fretted by the fret hand.

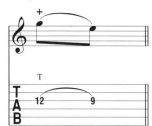

NATURAL HARMONIC: Strike the note while the fret-hand lightly touches the string directly over the fret indicated.

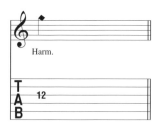

PINCH HARMONIC: The note is fretted normally and a harmonic is produced by adding the edge of the thumb or the tip of the index finger of the pick hand to the normal pick attack.

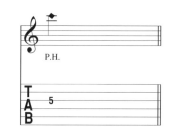

HARP HARMONIC: The note is fretted normally and a harmonic is produced by gently resting the pick hand's index finger directly above the indicated fret (in parentheses) while the pick hand's thumb or pick assists by plucking the appropriate string.

PICK SCRAPE: The edge of the pick is rubbed down (or up) the string, producing a scratchy sound.

MUFFLED STRINGS: A percussive sound is produced by laying the fret hand across the string(s) without depressing, and striking them with the pick hand.

PALM MUTING: The note is partially muted by the pick hand lightly touching the string(s) just before the bridge.

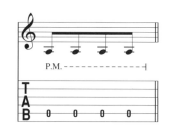

RAKE: Drag the pick across the strings indicated with a single motion.

TREMOLO PICKING: The note is picked as rapidly and continuously as possible.

ARPEGGIATE: Play the notes of the chord indicated by quickly rolling them from bottom to top.

VIBRATO BAR DIVE AND RETURN: The pitch of the note or chord is dropped a specified number of steps (in rhythm), then returned to the original pitch.

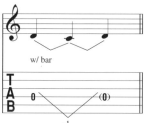

VIBRATO BAR SCOOP: Depress the bar just before striking the note, then quickly release the bar.

VIBRATO BAR DIP: Strike the note and then immediately drop a specified number of steps, then release back to the original pitch.

Additional Musical Definitions

(accent)	• Accentuate note (play it louder).	
(accent)	• Accentuate note with great intensity.	
(staccato)	• Play the note short.	
⊓	• Downstroke	
V	• Upstroke	
D.S. al Coda	• Go back to the sign (℅), then play until the measure marked "*To Coda*," then skip to the section labelled "**Coda**."	
D.C. al Fine	• Go back to the beginning of the song and play until the measure marked "*Fine*" (end).	

Rhy. Fig.	• Label used to recall a recurring accompaniment pattern (usually chordal).
Riff	• Label used to recall composed, melodic lines (usually single notes) which recur.
Fill	• Label used to identify a brief melodic figure which is to be inserted into the arrangement.
Rhy. Fill	• A chordal version of a Fill.
tacet	• Instrument is silent (drops out).
	• Repeat measures between signs.
	• When a repeated section has different endings, play the first ending only the first time and the second ending only the second time.

NOTE: Tablature numbers in parentheses mean:
1. The note is being sustained over a system (note in standard notation is tied), or
2. The note is sustained, but a new articulation (such as a hammer-on, pull-off, slide or vibrato) begins, or
3. The note is a barely audible "ghost" note (note in standard notation is also in parentheses).

237

STRUM AND PICK PATTERNS

This chart contains the suggested strum and pick patterns that are referred to by number at the beginning
of each song in this book. The symbols ⊓ and ∨ in the strum patterns refer to down and up strokes, respectively.
The letters in the pick patterns indicate which right-hand fingers play which strings.

p = thumb
i = index finger
m = middle finger
a = ring finger

For example; Pick Pattern 2
is played: thumb - index - middle - ring

Strum Patterns   Pick Patterns

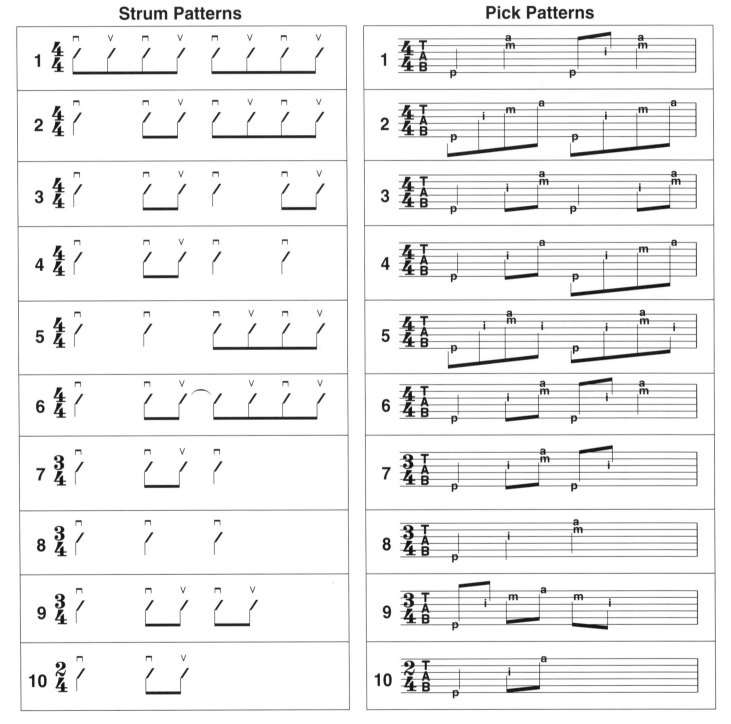

You can use the 3/4 Strum and Pick Patterns in songs written in compound meter (6/8, 9/8, 12/8, etc.).
For example, you can accompany a song in 6/8 by playing the 3/4 pattern twice in each measure.
The 4/4 Strum and Pick Patterns can be used for songs written in cut time (¢) by doubling the note
time values in the patterns. Each pattern would therefore last two measures in cut time.

238